Discipline
&
Discovery

Albert
Edward
Day

Discipline & Discovery

Albert Edward Day

Copyright © 1961, 1988 by
The Disciplined Order of Christ
Printed in the United States of America
ISBN: 0-88368-203-6

First Edition—1947
Revised—1961
Revised—1976
Revised—1988

Editorial assistance by Debra Petrosky.
Cover design by Cindy Feustal.

Unless otherwise noted, Scripture quotations are taken from the King James Version of the Bible.

Scripture quotations from the Revised Standard Version Bible, copyright 1946, 1952, 1971 by the Division of Christian Education of the National Council of the Churches of Christ in the U.S.A. are used by permission.

Contents

"The Living Christ"
by Howard W. Ellis

Dr. Howard W. Ellis, long-time friend and co-worker of Albert Edward Day, served on the New Life Mission staff from its inception in 1946.

The New Life movement, spearheaded by Dr. Albert Day, was a nationwide three-fold thrust involving the mission, the *New Life* magazine, and what has now become "The Disciplined Order of Christ". This spiritual growth movement was inaugurated and sponsored by the General Board of Evangelism of the Methodist Church.

Known far and wide for his Gospel in Art ministry, Howard Ellis' sketch of the head of Christ adorned the first edition of *Discipline And Discovery*, and we are pleased to present it again in the latest revision of this outstanding work.

Preface

Discipline And Discovery first appeared in 1947, and its sale and use have grown steadily ever since. Each year finds new readers and students turning its pages and, we hope, practicing its disciplines. Those who have known it longest prize it most. Testimony to its value in the training for the spiritual life continues to come from people around the world.

The years of discipline and discovery have taught us new lessons in this area, and they have been incorporated in this book. As we release this revised version, we pray the blessing of God on those who long to discover the joy of the disciplined life.

Albert Edward Day

7

On Discipline

1

On Discipline

As Christians, we are an undisciplined people.
That is the reason for the lack of spiritual insight
and moral power in the church today. We have for-
gotten the faithful practices that have given to
Christendom some of its noblest saints.

Without discipline there would have been no
Francis of Assisi, no Bernard of Clairvaux, no
Teresa of Avila, no Brother Lawrence, no William
Law, no Evelyn Underhill, no Thomas Kelly.

Without discipline we will fail to hand our suc-
cessors the baton of a rich spiritual legacy that
preceeding generations have skillfully placed
within our grasp.

The Need Of The Hour

The spiritual power of the church depends, not
upon complicated organization or creative
administration, important as these are; not upon
eloquent preaching nor adequate theology,

11

valuable as they are; not even upon unlimited financial resources.

What the Church primarily needs today, as always, is the presence of God-conscious, God-centered Christians. Even a few here and there would greatly help a church confronted by the chaos of this age.

A multitude of men and women, pressing "toward the mark for the prize of the high calling of God in Christ Jesus" (Philippians 3:14), would confront the secularism and scepticism of our time with a challenge not easily laughed off or cast aside.

True holiness is a witness that cannot be ignored. Real sainthood is a phenomenon to which even the worldly person pays tribute. The power of a life that exalts Christ would arrest and subdue those who are bored by our thin version of Christianity and churchmanship.

Co-Laboring With Christ

We have talked much of salvation by faith, but there has been little realization that all real faith involves discipline. Faith is not a blithe "turning it all over to Jesus." Faith is such confidence in Jesus that it takes seriously His summons, "If any man will come after me, let him deny himself, and take up his cross, and follow me" (Matthew 16:24).

We have loudly proclaimed our dependence upon the grace of God, never guessing that the *grace* of God is given only to those who practice the *grace of self-mastery*. "Work out your own salvation with fear and trembling; for God is at work in you both to will and to work for his good pleasure" (Philippians 2:12,13 *RSV*). Human beings working out, God working in—that is the New Testament synthesis.

If we omit either we will fail to become the saints so sorely needed in these times.

God has not abandoned us to human effort and determination in our practice of these disciplines. We can be assured that the indwelling power of the Holy Spirit "helpeth our infirmities" (Romans 8:26) and enables us to do the will of God.

On the other hand, what effect can the redeeming power of Almighty God have in the lives of persons who offer no disciplined cooperation? Those who will not lift their faces from the dust or shake off the shackles of their egocentric selves will doubtless remain in bondage to their sins and earthiness.

Real discipline is not vain effort to save one's self. It is an intelligent application to the self of those principles which enable the self to enter into life-giving fellowship with God who is our salvation.

Paul's Example

In all Christian literature there is no writer who had a clearer conviction concerning the salvation

13

provided only in Christ than Paul. His self-despair ended in that marvelous, ageless insight, "I thank God, through Jesus Christ our Lord" (Romans 7:25). "I know whom I have believed," he cries in an ecstasy of confident gladness, "and am persuaded that he is able" (2 Timothy 1:12). Paul was a salvationist in the noblest sense.

Paul was also a disciplinarian. "I keep under [subdue] my body, and bring it into subjection" (1 Corinthians 9:27).

"They that are Christ's have crucified the flesh with the affections and lusts" (Galatians 5:24).

"So fight I, not as one that beateth the air" (1 Corinthians 9:26).

"Mortify therefore your members which are upon the earth" (Colossians 3:5).

"Let us lay aside every weight and the sin which doth so easily beset us" (Hebrews 12:1).

"No man that warreth entangleth himself with the affairs of this life" (2 Timothy 2:4).

These are not the words of a man who scorned discipline!

Paul's statements are spontaneous evidence of the disciplines which he, trusting in Christ, imposed upon himself in his eager effort to give Christ the cooperation He needed to make Paul useful to the glory of God.

We must recover the significance and the necessity of the spiritual disciplines if we are to be fit for the Master's use. Without the disciplines we hold Christ at arm's length, who, while desiring to use us to save our society from disintegration and death, chooses not to violate the will of self-satisfied humanity.

The Goal Of This Book

This book was prepared primarily for the members of the Disciplined Order of Christ who have pledged themselves to disciplined lives. (See Appendix.) Many others over the years have been helped by it in their quest for intimate fellowship with God.

This book is intended to be a practical, day-by-day help for seekers of God. It will be, therefore, less descriptive and more directive.

One by one we will consider the important disciplines, and after a simple analysis of the character and necessity of each, we will give directions as to their practice.

In other words, here is a simple brochure on how to practice the disciplines of the spiritual life. It comes out of some familiarity with the lives of those who have walked the path of sainthood and is an effort to share with you the practices which a novice such as the author has found helpful. You are invited to journey with countless others as we set our faces toward the spiritual heights ahead.

What These Disciplines Are Not

2
What These Disciplines Are Not

It is very important that we have a clear understanding of the purpose of the disciplines we are about to undertake.

We certainly are not going to practice any of them under the illusion that we are piling up merit for ourselves. They do not help us accumulate spiritual capital on which we may draw at any time. They do not offset deficits which may have occurred through our surrender to temptation, nor do they make up for our failure to do some good deed.

No matter what we do by way of self-denial or self-dedication, we are always in debt to the perfect will of God. Remember the word of Jesus, "When ye shall have done all those things which are commanded you, say, We are unprofitable servants" (Luke 17:10). At the end of every day, or every hour, we are "in the red" on our balance sheet with God.

Not For Bargaining

There is nothing smacking of a commercial transaction between us and God involved in these disciplines. We are not traders in the celestial market—so much humility for so much heaven, so much purity for so much peace, so much simplicity for so much serenity. We cannot buy eternal life. That is the gift of God. The moment we permit any attitude of bargaining to enter into our disciplines we have ruined them and damaged our own souls.

"Blessed are the poor in spirit" (Matthew 5:3). One does not feel poor in spirit when one has paid for something because value has been given for value. The very notion that we can ever pay God for anything is revolting. As if God needed something from us—and, in providing it, we become for that moment God's equals if not God's benefactors! God makes no profit out of us but is always the loser in commerce with us.

Not For Earning Salvation

These disciplines are not a way of earning salvation. Nothing in the computation of our moral and spiritual wealth can ever be listed as "earned income." None of us ever "gets what is coming to us." If we did, we would never know the "riches of the glory of his inheritance in the saints'' (Ephesians 1:18). It is only the everlasting mercy that admits us into the company of God, here or yonder.

Not Atonement For Others

These disciplines should not be regarded as a sacrificial suffering by which we may help atone for the sins of others. They are not our way of sharing the redeeming agonies of Christ.

The Cure d' Ars used to scourge his body with steel whips and barbed chains in order that thereby his parishioners might be saved. He told a fellow priest that he had offered up his body for the sins of his flock. We do not think in such terms as that.

There is, however, a redemptive value in the disciplines we suggest. We undertake them not for ourselves only but for others. But it is not *our* agony that saves *them*; it is the divine quality of our life. It is God in us, it is our God-likeness that awakens and inspires them. The value of the disciplines is in their contribution to our own realization of God. Once God becomes real to us, others will begin to believe that God is real because of us.

Not For Private Salvation

These disciplines are not a technique for the achievement of a private salvation. Since we are persons, any salvation that truly saves us is a personal salvation. But personal salvation and private salvation are by no means synonymous.

St. Paul, John Wesley, St. Francis, John Knox, Catherine of Siena, and Evelyn Underhill of London experienced a truly personal salvation. But what happened to them was far from being a private affair.

Any religious experience that truly saves someone inevitably carries over into social relationships. If what has happened to that person does not make one a better spouse, a more conscientious citizen, a more generous employer, or a more reliable employee, then there is no salvation, only emotionalization.

Private salvation is a contradiction of terms. It is like black white or hateful love or lying truth. White cannot be black nor love hateful nor truth false. Neither can salvation be private.

William James used to insist that every concept be tested by the question, ''What sensible difference to anybody will its truth make?'' It is a fair test to apply to anybody's claim to salvation. What sensible difference has it made? Can one's family, neighbors, business associates, employees, or supervisors detect any difference?

No one has been saved unless the self that is at war with other selves has been crucified, and in its place a new self has been born—a self that loves all other selves with the very love with which Christ loves them.

22

It is to hasten the death of the egocentric self that these disciplines are recommended. Here in part is that "working out" which makes it possible for God to "work in us" to achieve God's blessed purpose for us and for all who are affected by our lives.

Our Minds And Hearts

3

Our Minds And Hearts

Because of the condition of our minds, God is not real to most of us. Yet God is closer than our own thoughts. God is nearer to our hearts than our own feelings. God is more intimate with our wills than our most vigorous decisions.

If we are not aware of the Creator, it is not because we are alone. It is, in part, because our mind is so under the sway of other interests that it cannot turn to God with the loving attention that might discern God's presence.

Did you ever encounter on the street a friend who looked at you without seeing you? You walked right into your friend before you were recognized. Your friend then confessed to such absorption in thought that you were not noticed until your intentional collision. You were there, yet you were not seen. Though actually in your presence, your friend was as unconscious of you as if you did not exist.

Gaining A Conscious Awareness of God

We can be so preoccupied by lesser realities that we do not sense the presence of the divine reality surrounding and sustaining us. Something has to happen to end that absorption in other affairs, so that we can turn our attention to God.

Sometimes events will do it. One encounters God in a crisis that brings a person to one's senses. Death, disaster, sickness, and the collapse of friendship are like the collision on the street. They shatter the tyranny of an idea or a dream and release us to the awareness of something greater— the reality of God.

To become aware of people only in our collisions with them betrays a shallow existence. A far greater tragedy is to notice God only in those events that shatter our habitual thoughts and dreams, compelling us to recognize God's presence and activity.

What makes life splendid is the constant awareness of God. What transforms the spirit into divine likeness is intimate fellowship with God. We are saved—from our pettiness and earthiness and selfishness and sin—by conscious communion with the Creator's greatness, love, and holiness.

We could not have such communion if God were not always at hand and eager for it. Neither can we have it unless we break the tyrannies which now divert our attention toward other and lesser matters.

What those tyrannies are may be summed up in three words—ego, things, people.

Self

The *ego* is just the self that is unduly concerned with self. It is the something within that overemphasizes I, me, and mine. It makes us measure issues, projects, causes, people, and even God by their effect upon *our* hopes, *our* plans, *our* profit, and *our* security.

If you want to measure the ego's tyranny over your mind, try to think of God for five minutes and see if even for that brief period you can keep I, me, and mine out of your thoughts. Only after long discipline can anybody give God that long, loving attention that makes close, conscious communion with the divine Self possible.

Things

Things tyrannize us, too. Money, clothes, houses, furniture, food, automobiles—all the material paraphernalia of existence—captivate our interests and dominate our thoughts. "To have" concerns us a great deal more than "to be." Few of us have attained the freedom from things that can truthfully sing,

> *A tent or a cottage,*
> *Why should I care?*

29

The proof of our "thing-mindedness" is, again, very easy. Try for five minutes to give God loving attention, which is the essence of true prayer. You will find your mind reverting over and over to things—to what you are wearing or what you would like to wear, to what you had for breakfast or what you want for lunch, to the salary you receive or the increase you are seeking, to the house you live in or the house you are trying to find, to the condition of your car or the prospect of a new one! With amazing frequency, things in some fashion will insert themselves into your brief effort to keep your mind fixed on God.

People

People exercise a disturbing lordship over our lives. What they think of us agitates us more than what God thinks of us. What they say to us or about us constantly preys upon our minds. We court their favor much more consistently than we seek to please God.

When we vigorously lash out against others, we reveal in the very persistence and vigor of our anathemas that people have "gotten to us". If these antagonists did not seem so large in our concerns, we would be much less aroused by what they have said and done to us. Our denunciations betray our own over-anxiety about other's good opinion. Efforts to set people in their place reveal how large a place they have seized in our attention.

If you really want to know whether you are under the dominion of people, try to commune with God for another five minutes and see whether in that very short period of time you can keep your thoughts absolutely centered on God. You will be dismayed to find how people will come crowding into your efforts at communion— the longing for people, the fear of people, the memory of people's words, the regret at people's actions, the anxiety over people's attitudes toward you.

Our Need For Deliverance

This tyranny of the ego and of things and of people must be broken. Otherwise we will not achieve that uninterrupted awareness of God by which we are transformed into divine likeness. When we can "enter into the closet and shut the door"—not the door of the closet merely, but the door of the mind—against everything and everyone else but God, then we are really engaging in that kind of prayer which is life-changing.

Only God can effect the final emancipation of our minds from these tyrants. Without God's delivering grace we will always be slaves. "O wretched man that I am! who shall deliver me from the body of this death? I thank God through Jesus Christ our Lord" (Romans 7:24,25).

Our Need To Work With God

The extent to which God can help us is limited without our cooperation. God must have our cooperation in dealing with us. God desires to feed, clothe, and heal us. God eagerly wants us to know the truth, but God cannot provide any of the real values of life unless we provide intelligent cooperation.

God wants to enter into communion with us. Oh, how God wants us! The cry of a lover for the beloved is nothing in comparison with the cry of God for us. But, God can never have us nor can we have God unless we are willing to undertake the practices that will help God help us out of the tenacious, earthy entanglements of our own minds.

Does God Have Your Attention?

One of the rare and wonderful spirits of our time, Simone Weil, blessed as she was with an insight born out of years of disciplined attention to God, wrote that "one quarter of an hour of attention is worth any quantity of good works."

She adds: "After months of inner darkness, I suddenly and irrevocably acquired the certitude that all human beings, even if their natural faculties are almost nil, can penetrate into the realm of truth reserved to genius, if only they desire the truth and are willing to make an unceasing effort to achieve it . . . the quantity of creative genius in any epoch is strictly proportionate to the quantity of extreme attention."

Prayer has been simply but unforgettably described as "loving attention to God." The Scriptures have always urged us to fix our attention on God.

"Thou wilt keep him in perfect peace, whose mind is stayed on thee" (Isaiah 26:3).

"Keep thy heart with all diligence; for out of it are the issues of life" (Proverbs 4:23).

"Whatsoever things are true . . . think on these things" (Philippians 4:8).

"Looking unto Jesus the author and finisher of our faith" (Hebrews 12:2).

In these and many other passages, it is both stated and implied that we must change the direction of our attention and so alter the content of our own thought life.

There is a ceaseless interaction between body and mind, between what we do and what we think. The person whose actions are always in self-interest cannot develop an interest in others. The person whose conduct is persistently related to the accumulation of things will never relate easily to God. What we do outside of prayer, we will be when we pray.

Jesus emphasizes that: "Why *call* ye me, Lord, Lord, and *do not* the things which I say?" (Luke 6:46). The only way we can make Him Lord of our entire life is by doing the things that are a recognition of His lordship.

"Whosoever heareth these sayings of mine, and doeth them, I will liken him unto a wise man, which built his house upon a rock" (Matthew 7:24). It is the doing that gives a rock-like stability to the support of a godly life.

The Soil Of Our Hearts

The parable of the sower (Mark 4:3-8) vividly portrays the condition of one's heart and the efforts of God to help us. In this parable the condition of the soil determined the fate of the seed and the absence or abundance of a crop. In life, the condition of our hearts determines the fate of the truth which God sends to us.

A hard, materialized heart, like wayside soil, gives God no access. A heart that is shallow, like thin soil on stony ground, gives a quick response, but offers no sustenance to God's truth and therefore no harvest. A heart absorbed in many mundane concerns, like thorny ground, soon chokes the spiritual aspirations to death. Only the heart that is clean, simple, and cultivated, like a plowed, weeded field, can receive and nurture the truth of God and reap a harvest of godly character.

Just as the farmer is responsible for the condition of the soil, so are we responsible for the condition of our hearts. The disciplines here proposed are the plowing, weeding, and cultivating essential to the development of a heart that will be capable of receiving God.

The Goal Of These Disciplines

Let me repeat again—these disciplines are not a humanistic scheme of salvation. They are a simple description and prescription of techniques that will help us to open the way for the triune God, in whom alone is there salvation for any of us.

These techniques are time-tested. If they seem like novelties, it is because our teachers have failed to acquaint us with what the saints have demonstrated over and over again.

Give them a thorough trial as the members of the Disciplined Order of Christ are pledged to do. You are entreated not to miss the values that the disciplines offer.

It is suggested that from here on, you limit yourself to one chapter a week. Read the chapter, meditate on it, and master it. Then daily practice the disciplines as they are printed in the calendar at the end of each chapter.

An intelligent mastery and faithful practice of these disciplines are the certain road to communion with God.

God bless us all as we journey together.

Obedience

4
Obedience

"True and perfect obedience is a virtue above all virtues."

That affirmation by Meister Eckhart would be approved by saints of all ages. No virtue can surpass obedience in its ministry to the life with God. It is the condition of all other virtues. No one who is disobedient can be pure or truthful or just or generous. Everyone who has learned to obey is more certain to acquire all the other qualities that equip the soul for companionship with God.

The significance of obedience is not merely that it makes for social order, nor that it brings us into line with God's perfect will. Actually, obedience is a vigorous blow against one of the tyrants that monopolize us—our ego.

The Strength Of The Ego

Obedience means assent to another's right to command and specific consent to that command.

Such assent and consent smite the ego and our self-ish pride.

One of the most constant characteristics of the ego is its desire to "run the show." It insists on being boss. "No one is going to tell me what to do" is its most common utterance. It resents restrictions of any kind. "No smoking allowed" is only an inspiration to smoke. "No parking here" is a challenge to park right there and nowhere else. It refuses to be "told." Its perpetual and persistent demand is for the right of self-expression and self-determination.

If you want to discover how strong your own ego is, ask yourself whom you ever obey. Whom? Certainly not the church! If you keep its rules, it is usually because they happen to coincide with your desires. The church to which I belong has a significant body of general rules. Few of them are honored by consistent obedience. Many of them are just ignored. Some are laughed to scorn.

Do you obey the State? Yes, sometimes. But not when disobedience has a chance at immunity. What about traffic laws, for example? Do you ever look in the mirror and then step on the gas? Do stop signs stop you? Do traffic lanes control you?

Do you obey God without rationalizing away the real meaning of God's commands? The Scriptures say, "speak evil of no one" (Titus 3:2 *RSV*). Do you refrain, or under the pretext of ferreting out wrong, do you let your tongue dwell on a morsel of gossip?

Jesus says, "First take the log out of your own eye, and then you will see clearly to take out the speck from your brother's eye" (Luke 6:42 *RSV*). Have you ever really touched the log, or do you always pick away at the speck under the guise of being helpful? God says, "Love your enemies" (Matthew 5:44). Do you—or do you merely leave them alone? Quite a difference there!

The Nature Of Obedience

Obedience is not a habit with most people because the ego is on the throne and refuses to vacate. Every act of obedience is a blow at this usurper. Continuous efforts at obedience gradually undermine the ego's tyranny. Perfect obedience would mean that the tyrant is dead.

Obedience is both an art and an ever new adventure. By practice it becomes easier. Yet every new situation makes new demands that can be met only by creative consecration. Yesterday's obedience is never quite adequate for today, but it does make today's obedience more likely.

We need not fear that the wise practice of obedience will make mere puppets out of us. Rather, it makes the real self more truly master. When the usurping ego is manacled and finally banished, the real self, made in the image of God, is able to act like a child of God. One becomes a true person when, recognizing God as Lord, both freedom and fulfillment are found in that lordship.

41

The Practice of Obedience

If the practice is to achieve the results we are seeking—namely, the ending of the ego's tyranny—then it must involve obedience at the points where the ego is most insistent upon its own way. All obedience to rightful commands is helpful. But one might easily spend his time obeying the lesser, and totally neglect the more important ones. So often we

> *Compound for sins we are inclined to*
> *by leaving those we have no mind to.*

As long as we leave the ego unchallenged at the place of its strongest desires, it matters little what we do about its slight preferences and lesser inclinations.

Each one of us, therefore, must deal frankly and ruthlessly with our own ego. What may be a difficult veto for someone else may be an easy one for you. Where another finds it easy to say no, you may have your greatest difficulty. We are going to offer some suggested acts of obedience. Necessarily they will be only a few of the more general ones. Specific acts, which the condition of your ego may demand, will have to be discovered by yourself.

Do not fail to make that discovery. The clue to it is in your own affinities and revulsions. They are not found in your opinions, for they may be the rationalization of your desires, but are found in your impulses and yearnings and aversions. Wherever strong feelings are involved, there is the place to begin on your ego.

Whenever a command from God or other rightful authority arouses an inner rebellion, then is the time for you to make certain that you do not rebel but obey! Unless you do, you are giving the tyrant a longer lease at the very point where his hold is strongest. *Always remember, where the emotion is deepest, there the ego is most staunchly in command.*

Do not, therefore, turn away from any of the suggested practices simply because they upset you. You need to be upset. Only then can the throne be emptied of its present occupant and the rightful ruler crowned.

On the other hand, do not scorn any of these suggested practices because they arouse no storm and create no sense of difficulty. Remember that obedience to any lawful authority is good. It can do you no harm. It will certainly aid you in destroying the tyrants that distract you from transforming fellowship with God.

The practices will be divided among the days of the week. Emphasize them in turn, but keep as many of them in mind as can be done without enslaving the memory. Remember, these are not legalistic requirements. They are devices for keeping alive in you the *spirit* of obedience.

—Recall some rules of the church and faithfully practice them today.

—Attend a service whether you feel like it or not.

—Bow your head in prayer when entering your pew, even though you may be curious to see who else is present.

—Maintain reverent silence even though your neighbor insists on whispered conversation.

—Pay your church pledge in full.

—Join in the singing and the prayers.

—Move over and graciously let someone else have the end seat.

—Greet some strangers warmly, even though you would rather step away quietly.

—For today, refrain from "uncharitable and unprofitable conversation," "foolish talking and jesting." You may not quite see the point. But here is a rule, obey it.

—Obey your own highest ideals for this one day.

—Read one chapter of the Sermon on the Mount and faithfully conform your conduct to the spirit and purpose of that teaching. Do not argue today, but obey, obey, obey.

If the preacher's sermon made clear even one injunction of Christ, see if you can fulfill it to the letter for this one day.

In the course of the day, you may remember a number of lessons that the preaching, teaching, and reading of other days impressed upon you.

As they emerge in memory, obey them. See if you can go through the entire day without one act of disobedience to the remembered standards of Christ.

Monday

Today the labors of the week will be resumed. You will be thrown into atmospheres and associations unlike those of a quiet Sunday. The challenges to your conscience will be different, too—and in some ways more difficult. But think of them as opportunities to carry on your conquest of the ego by obedience even amid the general disobedience that surrounds you.

—Begin today with an act of obedience such as kneeling in homage before God or offering special thanksgiving for the opportunities of another week of labor or getting up half an hour earlier than usual in order to spend the time in prayer.

—Let the other members of the family have the first chance at the morning paper or the pancakes from the kitchen, in fulfillment of the command, "Thou shalt love thy neighbour as thyself" (Matthew 22:39). Maybe they are not in the same hurry you are, but you will still have time to get to your work.

—When you drive to your factory or office observe the traffic laws; keep the required speed; stay in your own lane; give the right of way to those entitled to it; don't crowd the light signals.

It isn't merely a question of safety but of schooling yourself by obedience.

—If you are in an office remember the rule, "Let each of you look not only to his own interests but also to the interests of others" (Philippians 2:4 *RSV*). Don't do it to criticize others, but to discover where you can be helpful. You may have a heavy burden to carry, but do not let the day pass without lifting someone else's burden. "Bear ye one another's burdens and so fulfil the law of Christ" (Galatians 6:2). You may not be inclined to add someone else's burden to your own, but that is all the more reason why you should.

—If you are in a factory, remember the words of the apostle Paul, "Whatever your task, work heartily, as serving the Lord and not men" (Colossians 3:23 *RSV*). Your wage may be inadequate, your employer thoughtless, your working conditions anything but pleasant. Do your job as speedily and skillfully as you can. Make your work area an altar. You are obeying God, not merely a human being or a company.

—If you are at home, the day will bring many challenges to your ego. Requests, if not orders, will come from other members of the family. You can ignore them or evade them or flatly repudiate them. Or you can obey under the compulsion of a spirit that realizes the value of having something to obey every day.

Remember this passage from the New Testament:

Submitting yourselves one to another in the fear of God. Wives, submit yourselves unto your own husbands, as unto the Lord. For the husband is the head of the wife, even as Christ is the head of the church: and he is the saviour of the body. Therefore as the church is subject unto Christ, so let the wives be to their own husbands in every thing. Husbands, love your wives, even as Christ also loved the church, and gave himself for it; that he might sanctify and cleanse it with the washing of water by the word, that he might present it to himself a glorious church, not having spot, or wrinkle, or any such thing; but that it should be holy and without blemish. So ought men to love their wives as their own bodies. He that loveth his wife loveth himself. For no man ever yet hated his own flesh; but nourisheth and cherisheth it, even as the Lord the church: for we are members of his body, of his flesh, and of his bones. For this cause shall a man leave his father and mother, and shall be joined unto his wife, and they two shall be one flesh. This is a great mystery: but I speak concerning Christ and the church. Nevertheless let every one of you in particular so love his wife even as himself;

and the wife see that she reverence her
husband—Ephesians 5:21-33.

Tuesday

One marvelous area in which to develop habits
of obedience and to practice the disciplines of obedience is in the realm of our human relationships.
Try the following for today:

—Let the reasonable wishes of your friends
become to you a law. Do not question. Do not discuss. Obey.

—If you are serving on a committee, be content
to defer to the wishes of others, providing of
course that those wishes involve no wrong.

—When the vexed bus driver orders you to move
to the rear, move quietly and without protest.

—If the clerk asks you to try on a coat, even
though you are sure you do not want that one, try
it on without a gesture of annoyance.

—If some driver, by blaring his horn, gives you
the command to move over and let him or her
pass, then move. Even though you have been asked
what no law requires, obey the impatient driver
as readily as you would a policeman. That would
be an especially good dose for your ego.

—While waiting in line to pay for food at the
store, someone, by an elbow or a wiggle, may vir-
tually ask you to step back one place. Do it. That
may be the most noteworthy act of obedience you
have performed for many a day.

—If this is election day, vote! That is your plain duty. Obey it.

Wednesday

Suppose today you begin with a fresh study of the teachings of Jesus. If you are looking for commands, you can find none comparable. Get a good commentary if you can. Open the Bible to Matthew 5, and read a paragraph. Meditate on its meaning and then say yes to it in your thoughts, words, and deeds today.

—"Blessed are the poor in spirit" (Matthew 5:3). That means you will toss overboard any signs of complacency or self-satisfaction.

—"Blessed are they that mourn" (Matthew 5:4). That means you will manifest genuine concern over your spiritual poverty.

—"Blessed are the meek" (Matthew 5:5). Some think that means "the disciplined." If so, then faithfully practice the disciplines you know.

—"Blessed are the merciful" (Matthew 5:7). Let not one hour pass today without some act of mercy on your part: the forgiveness of some offender; the gracious courtesy to someone who may not deserve it; the modification of some claim you have against another; the giving to someone an undeserved kindness.

These are only a few of the demands that will come to you as you prayerfully read the Bible. Obey, obey, obey.

Thursday

Examine your acts of obedience earlier in the week, by asking yourself such questions as these:

—Did I obey wholly or only in part?

—Did I obey wholly but imperfectly?

—Did I obey in my own way or in the spirit of the command?

—Did I obey on first command or did I need a second or third?

—Did I obey cheerfully or with reluctance?

—Did I go slowly and lazily or quickly and energetically about my task?

It will be quite sufficient for this day if you carefully watch your obedience and amend it in the light of the above questions.

"Be ye therefore perfect, even as your Father which is in heaven is perfect" (Matthew 5:48).

Friday

Today study your usual or special obedience in the light of other questions.

—Do I obey carelessly and without due attention or thoughtfully and with a real effort to be diligent?

—Do I obey only after some argument or at once without contradiction?

—Do I obey complainingly or cheerfully?

—Do I obey dejectedly or hopefully with happy expectancy?

—Do I obey readily in matters that seem of great consequence, but reluctantly in trivial affairs?

—Do I obey in form but not in spirit?

—Do I always try to excuse myself on the grounds of inability or do I fling myself into the obedience and trust the result with God?

—Do I try to persuade the one who gives the command into recalling it or do I act as those whose function is "*not to make reply; Theirs but to do and die*"?

These questions will greatly improve the quality and significance of our obedience.

Saturday

By today we may be rather weary, our tempers a bit short, and our nerves crying for the rest of Sunday. Obedience will come harder; resentment and rebellions, easier.

Therefore, today may be the day of greatest importance—for an obedience freely, cheerfully, efficiently given will represent a greater conquest of the ego than anything that has happened earlier in the week.

So for today be unusually alert to hear the commands that will come—especially from within.

When he calls me, I will answer. I'll be somewhere listening for my name.

It may come quietly, so quietly you will miss

51

it if you are not listening. It may touch the ego on an especially sensitive spot. Let it be your effort to bring the week to a triumphant close by such ready obedience to the inner voice that the new week will dawn with a sense of victory.

If the week has left you with a sense of defeat, let that be a lesson in humility. It is not difficult to continue any discipline when one has been able to practice it victoriously. The real challenge to obedience comes when, having tried to obey and failed, one keeps on trying.

Scripture Readings For The Week:

Sunday:	Obedience from the heart. *Romans 6:16-23*
Monday:	Action not promise. *Matthew 21:28-32*
Tuesday:	The best sacrifice. *1 Samuel 15:17-23*
Wednesday:	Obedience in thought. *2 Corinthians 10:1-5*
Thursday:	Obedience in Christ. *Philippians 2:1-10*
Friday:	Obedience to authority. *Titus 3:1-11*
Saturday:	Obedience at home. *Colossians 3:18-25*

Simplicity

5
Simplicity

Seldom do we hear anything about simplicity as an essential discipline of the spiritual life. Most of us have only a vague idea of the meaning of the word.

Perhaps we should begin with a definition. Simplicity is the "absence of artificial ornamentation, pretentious style, or luxury." It is "artlessness, lack of cunning or duplicity."

Where there is simplicity, words can be taken at face value. There are no hidden or double meanings. One says what one means and means what one says. There is no "joker" concealed in the language to nullify its obvious intent.

Simplicity does not mean "easy to understand." The apostle Paul was not always easy to understand nor was Jesus. People are still wrestling with their great utterances. But both Jesus and Paul were characterized by simplicity. Their intention was not to confuse or deceive but to clarify and illumine.

The Motive Of Simplicity

Where there is simplicity there is no artificiality. One does not try to appear younger, or wiser, or richer than one is—nor saintlier! Moffatt's translation of 1 Corinthians 13:4 hits it exactly in stating "Love makes no parade, gives itself no airs."

Where there is simplicity, there is no effort to get by cunning what one could not get if one's purpose were clear. One does not "act as if" one were seeking something other than one's real quest, or going elsewhere than one's real destination, or intending to do what one is not going to do.

Where there is simplicity, one does not constantly keep people guessing. The common adage affirms "in wit an adult: in simplicity a child." A child is obvious—until some of our guile is caught. You know the child's state of mind, its estimate of people, its intentions, and its desires.

Simplicity In Action

We once had in our home a guest of rarest spirit—so wise, so richly human, so saintly. We asked him to read the Bible and offer prayer before we rose from the table. We wanted our children to share the benediction of his wonderful spiritual life. He did read, in that deep, rich voice that was like the music of a great organ. He prayed as one who knew and loved God.

When the prayer was finished there was a

moment of silence, so hushed and awed were the souls of us who were older. But the silence was soon broken by the piping protest of our little boy. "My, that was a long one!" That was simplicity! So also was the chuckling laughter of our distinguished guest at the lad's naivete. He was not pretending either.

When our guest prayed, he was talking sincerely with a Friend. And then he laughed just as sincerely because the humor of the child's reaction stirred his sense of humor. He did not feel the need of appearing "shocked." Both the boy and the bishop had the grace of simplicity. Each was what he was in delightful artlessness.

Jesus said, "Whosoever shall not receive the kingdom of God as a little child, he shall not enter therein"(Mark 10:15). With this definition and interpretation, perhaps it is becoming clear how the practice of simplicity is an essential discipline.

Simplicity And The Ego

Remember now that we are trying to emancipate ourselves from the tyranny of the ego and things and people, so that we are free to turn toward God and to become aware of God and to have fellowship with God.

Simplicity will help us in our attack upon all three of these tyrants.

Simplicity is very effective in its impact upon the ambitious and aggressive nature of the ego.

57

The ego wants attention, recognition, and applause. You have laughed at its pushiness in others. In conventions, you have watched with amusement the delegates who must always be trotting to the platform to confer in impressive whispers with the presiding officer; or who must somehow get the floor even when they have nothing important to say; or who, when ostensibly arguing a serious issue, must put themselves and their achievements on parade.

Or, you have been amused at people who seem to be unhappy at any social gathering unless and until the conversation turns toward them as subjects of discussion or as leaders in it. Or, you have been disgusted at the efforts of some to get their names into print or into resolutions of appreciation or into "honorable mention" lists. If we assume that their egos are any more insistent and dominant than our own, we shall do them grave injustice and deceive ourselves.

If this ego, which bears our name, is not pushy in the ways we have just recalled, it is no shrinking violet. Make no mistake there. It wants attention and approval, too, and will resort to whatever means seems likely to get them.

Deflating The Ego

Here are some of the artful devices the ego employs:

It will wear clothes, join clubs, buy cars,

live in houses, and sport jewelry beyond its means in order to appear as a financial success.

It will go to extravagant lengths to seem to belong to the intelligentsia; use "big words" when more common words would say it better; read or listen to book reviews, but never sit down with the books themselves, in order to be able to comment on authors and writings and so gain a reputation as an "omnivorous reader". The ego will repeat observations, dropped by wise persons, as its own mature judgment on important issues; maintain a "discreet silence," not out of respect for those who have a right to talk but as an indication of superior knowledge too complex to be communicated to *that* group.

It will do many things that genuine piety does, if piety is "the thing" in its community or social group. Church membership is a badge of respectability in many places, so the ambitious ego is always looking for the church where ambition has the best chance of fulfillment.

There will be no conscious hypocrisy. The ego is quite too subtle for that. What happens is the taking on of religious practices that will evoke favorable comment, without making the commitments which link the life to God.

In these and many other ways, the ego with artfulness and cunning will press for the fulfillment of its ambitions. One who is realistic about oneself cannot fail to identify the varied and often astonishing subtleties whereby one's ego has sought or maintained a status to which it is not entitled.

When one begins to practice simplicity, the ego is deprived of the very strategy by which it sustains itself. Nothing will deflate the ego more effectively than to be recognized for what it is. It lives by pretension. It dies when the mask is torn away and the stark reality is exposed to the gaze of others.

If you doubt it, try it!

Simplicity And Things

Simplicity also avails in breaking the tyranny of things. Ostentation, artificiality, ornamentation, pretentious style, luxury—all require things. One requires few things to be one's self, one's age, and one's moral, intellectual, or spiritual stature. What one *is* does not depend upon what one *has*. If you are willing to be as old as you are, you need few cosmetics. If you are ready to occupy the place your intelligence, character, or spirituality deserves, you need neither a big house nor the latest model car, nor an elaborate wardrobe. It is amazing how much less a place things occupy in one's thinking when one is not under the necessity of achieving or maintaining status by erecting facades.

A very dear friend wrote the other day of the lovely tributes recently paid to him on the occasion of his departure for a new field of labor. He told how it humbled him to know that youth were looking to him for leadership. He added, "I must not fail to be what people think I am." I know what that will mean in his life—not the accumulation of *things,* in order to impress people that he is a success—but the study and prayer and disciplined living that will beget the intellectual, moral, and spiritual character on which people can depend and by which they can be inspired. His simplicity and sincerity, therefore, deliver him from any undue concern for things and devote him to spiritual quests.

Simplicity always functions in that direction. Being willing to be known for what we are, we are not under the constraint of resorting to *things* to conceal what we are or to convey an impression of greatness to those who are so easily impressed by the gadgets in which our civilization abounds.

Making A Good Impression

Simplicity also helps to deliver us from the tyranny of people. The effort to make an impression, of course, is born in an undue concern over what people think about us. We would not employ any artifice to make an impression if we were not so anxious about the impression we make. The opinion people have of us often looms larger in our thinking than becoming the kind of person who deserves their good opinion but who can be independent of their opinion, good or bad. Instead of becoming such a person, we resort to all sorts of devices to make them think we are that person.

Just as our emphasis should be not on "having" but on "being," so it should also be on "being" and not on "seeming." Then our attention will be not on other people but on our own personality. Then people will cease to dominate us.

The very presence of artfulness, of what students call "apple polishing," of flattery, of affectation, demonstrates that consciousness is under the tyranny of people. Whenever there is simplicity you know that tyranny is broken.

Only the simple are the free. All the rest are under the tyranny of the ambitious ego, its demand for recognition and for things, and its preoccupation with people.

Hence, only the simple are free to direct their attention to God steadily, uninterruptedly, and so enter into conscious, vivid, and redemptive fellowship with God. No wonder Jesus said, "Except ye be converted, and become as little children, ye shall not enter into the kingdom of heaven" (Matthew 18:3).

No wonder Lieberman observes: "Simplicity is the virtue of the perfect."

The Disciplines Of Simplicity

We should keep in mind the wise caution of Bede Frost: "We cannot, by observing rules, make ourselves simple. All we can do is to show our desire to remove the hindrances in our Lord's way, to empty ourselves so that we may be filled with the simplicity which is in Christ Jesus."

But humble as is the role we play, it is an important role. Only we can play it. God waits on humanity. That is the blessed truth. God waits and waits and waits. That is also the frightening truth. God must wait. God cannot act until we remove the hindrances.

> *O shame, thrice shame upon us,*
> *To keep Him standing there.*

Here are some simple things we can practice daily to open the way for God.

In our disciplines of obedience, we suggested some for each day in the week. As we seek simplicity, the day by day calendar will be dropped for sake of variety. A number of disciplines will be suggested, all of which may be employed on any one day. Or if one's case is particularly stubborn, one may take each of these disciplines and make it the practice for a day.

In all of these suggestions, flexibility of practice should be maintained. Rigid rules are the enemies of spirituality. But mere impulsive, haphazard behavior is also destructive. So use these suggestions, not as moral "big sticks," but as guides and stimuli to the behavior that will lead you into the liberty of Christ.

63

Simplicity In Word

Watch your language. Avoid exaggeration. In retelling a story do not "dress it up." Be sparing with your adjectives. We deceive more frequently with adjectives than with nouns or verbs. Be careful of your emphases. By emphasizing the wrong word or over-emphasizing any word or phrase, one can make a verbal truth an actual lie. Resist the temptation to make an event or an action or a decision sound bigger or more heroic than it actually was. Avoid seeking after an "effect." Say simply and clearly what you mean.

This may seem unimportant. It is, on the other hand, very important. If we are to practice simplicity it must begin with our speech. Jesus knew what was involved when He said, "Let your communication be, Yea, yea; Nay, nay," or as Moffatt translates it: "Let what you say be simply 'yes' or 'no'; whatever goes beyond that springs from evil" (Matthew 5:37). The apostle Paul adds: "Let your talk always have a saving salt of grace about it" (Colossians 4:6 *Moffatt*).

At the end of the day, review your conversation during the day, and ask yourself some pertinent questions about it. "Did I say exactly what I meant?" "Did I seek to create any false impression?" "Did I color any of my language for effect?" "Did I make any claim for myself, my knowledge, my skill, my actions, my intentions, my attitudes, and my relations that went beyond reality?''

Examine yourself as relentlessly as if it were someone else you were examining. Repent of your failure. Resolve, by the grace of Christ, not to fail in the same way tomorrow. Ask God to keep watch over the door of your lips. (See Psalm 141:3 *RSV.*)

Simplicity In Deed

Study your behavior! Be honest, now. Are your actions and your real self *one*? Are your doing, going, buying, and joining a facade which conceals the reality of your situation?

Are you living within your income? Are you pretending to be an expert where you are only an amateur? Do you really read the books to which you refer or from which you quote? Do you pray as often as you seem to? Is the Bible you carry under your arm on Sunday in your heart the rest of the week? Does your noisy orthodoxy testify to a life in harmony with God's will? Does your rather ostentatious heresy mean a real intellectual problem, or is it a cover for the relaxation of the claims of Christ on your life?

Maybe none of these questions comes close to you—though frankly that is doubtful. Even so, ask yourself some questions. Let the crux of each question be the sincerity, the artlessness, the simplicity of the behavior for which others praise you and you have been praising yourself!

Suggested Resolutions To Practice

—I will say exactly what I mean.

—I will not color my language for effect.

—I will not pretend that I know when I can only guess.

—I will keep silent when I do not know.

—I will say nothing to make anybody believe I am wiser or better than I know myself to be.

—I will not let my silence convey a false impression of myself or my convictions.

—I will be sparing in the use of adjectives.

—I will not use rhetoric as a curtain to conceal my mind.

—I will avoid making excuses for myself.

—I will avoid phrases with double and dubious meaning.

—I will conform my actions to reality.

—I will buy only what I can afford and what my responsibility to the underprivileged suggests.

—I will make my behavior a Bible to all who know me.

—I will claim no grace I do not possess but seek all the grace available in Christ.

—I will avoid all rationalization of my doubts, and pay, to the best I know, the homage of a sincere quest.

—I will make of my work a means of training in simplicity by the following:

Aiming at excellence in my work instead of concerning myself with what people may think or say;

Doing the best I can but without over-anxiety as to its perfection;

Doing one thing at a time;

Offering my work to God;

Letting God lead me in my work and outside of it.

Finally, when our examination reveals that by artful speech or silence or deed we have conveyed false impressions, it will be a valuable discipline if we do more than repent. We can go one step further and visit or write or telephone the person or persons involved and make an apology and correct the impression. Then we will not be so likely to fail in that same way again!

Scripture Readings For The Week:

Sunday:	Simplicity in giving. *Matthew 6:1-4*
Monday:	Simplicity in prayer. *Matthew 6:5-15*
Tuesday:	Simplicity in discipline. *Matthew 6:16-18*
Wednesday:	Childlike simplicity. *Mark 10:13-16*

Thursday:	Simplicity of speech.
	Matthew 5:33-37
Friday:	Simplicity of service.
	2 Corinthians
	1:12-14
Saturday:	The simplicity of
	Christ.
	2 Corinthians 11:1-3

Humility

6
Humility

This is not a popular word with us Americans.
We are known around the world for our boasting.
In a town in Oklahoma there is a little sprawling
laundry located along the highway. On the little
laundry is a large sign, easily read by the tourist
hastening to leave the town. The sign shakes its
fist, so to speak, at any city dweller inclined to
look with contempt on that town and its business.
It defiantly says, "This Is the Biggest Laundry of
Its Size in the World." What a characteristically
American assertion. No matter how small we are,
we are the biggest; no matter how illiterate, we
are the smartest; no matter how chaotic our moral
life, we are the best on earth!

We are so afraid of an inferiority complex that
we hesitate to admit any inferiority. We are bound
to believe in ourselves, even at the price of refus-
ing to believe in some standard that rebukes us.
Our code of behavior usually includes
assertiveness.

In politics and religion our opinions easily harden into dogmas. We are proud of our every accomplishment, resentful at criticism, and inclined to balance our envy at the success of others with a secret contempt for them as persons. We are confident we could do a better job than the President, write a better sermon than the preacher, manage our neighbor's children more efficiently than their parents do, and play a better game than the tired athletes battling imminent defeat on the gridiron.

We are not only proud but proud of our pride.

True And False Humility

We associate humility with weakness, confusing it with the sprawling mind and the flabby will. We think we find its supreme illustration in the person who seems almost to apologize for being alive. We believe that to be humble means to "crawl," to "lick the dust," to be lacking in self-respect, even to deny whatever goodness or skill or truth one possesses.

All of which means that we are deceived both as to the reality of our own lives and as to the nature of real humility. If we were as wonderful as we think we are, we should think we are a lot less wonderful than we do.

True greatness is always humble. An American girl was being shown about the house of Mendelssohn, the great musician. At last she stood before the piano at which the master had composed so many of his great pieces. With unabashed eagerness she blurted, "It would be a thrill to play Mendelssohn's piano. May I?" Her guide was annoyed but consented. She sat down without embarrassment or any evidence of reverence and proceeded to play. She satisfied her craving for the thrill that would come when she could return to America and say, "What do you think? I played on Mendelssohn's piano!"

Then she turned to her guide and said, "I believe you play, too. Sit down and give us a number." But the guide, himself a musician of no small ability, bowed and replied: "No, madam, I am not worthy to touch the keys over which Mendelssohn's magic fingers once roamed."

True greatness is always humble! Our lack of humility is not due to our excess of ability but to our woeful failure to appraise ourselves in the light of the Master's life!

That is what true humility is—not the denial of whatever excellence or ability we may possess, but such a vision of the divine excellence and power that ours seems but dust and ashes in comparison.

In one of the greatest books of the Middle Ages, *Holy Wisdom,* Father Baker describes the humility that is morally real and spiritually wholesome: "This same humility is to be exercised . . . in the quiet, loving sight of the infinite, endless being and goodness of Jesus. . . . Such a beholding will work in thy mind a far more pure, spiritual, solid, and

73

perfect humility. . . . Thou wilt see and feel thyself . . . in the very substance of thy soul to be mere nothing" (p. 60).

Such humility is or should be "a standing order . . . framed, glazed, and hung up in the council chamber of the soul," as Rickaby so truly declares. It is, as Teresa devoutly affirmed, "the principal aid to prayer."

The reason ought to be clear to any one who has read thus far in this manual. Prayer at its best is transforming communion with God. God is always ready for such communion. Often we are not ready because of tyrannies that divert our minds to lesser matters.

The Problem Of The Ego

The worst tyranny of all is that of the ego. It makes us egocentric instead of God-centric—self-conscious instead of God-conscious. When we kneel in prayer our mind is so occupied with the desires and demands of our ego that we cannot truly turn to God.

"Ye shall seek me, and find me, when ye shall search for me with all your heart" (Jeremiah 29:13). But we don't. Our search is half-hearted, or even no-hearted. Most of the time we do not seek God at all. We are seeking something else— God is only incidental to the fulfillment of our egocentric wishes. We seek God only to make our selfish dreams come true.

"If a man goes seeking God and, with God, something else," says Meister Eckhart, "he will not find God. But if one seeks *only* God—and really so—he will never find only God but along with God, himself, he will find all that God is capable of."

The ego is always inserting its own desires into the search, and so it is forever spoiling the quest. Sometimes what it inserts seems very religious, almost holy. "Aware of it or not, people have wanted to have the great experiences; they want it in this form or they want that good thing; and this is nothing but self-will!" That is Eckhart again. But it is also life. That is why life is bereft of God.

For as still another great seer, Considine, avows, "It is self-importance, not our misery that gets in God's way." Very clearly, then, something must be done to this destructive and pervasive self-importance and self-will.

The Power Of Humility

Here is where humility is so effective. Self-importance vanishes and self-will disappears in the presence of humility. The humble person has dismissed self from the center of the picture. Personal welfare or even survival no longer seems to be the paramount issue. This person is perfectly willing to leave life's planning in the hands of God.

In prayer, thoughts turn readily and gladly away from oneself, one's notions and ambitions, desires and needs, to God. "I am nothing. I have nothing. I want only Thy name to be hallowed, Thy kingdom to come, Thy will to be done. Give me only what Thou wilt, when Thou wilt, as Thou wilt. I desire only Thee but if in Thy wisdom and love it seemeth best to withhold even Thyself from me, so be it, my Lord."

The Paradox Of Humility

To one who has not attained such a state, humility seems the negation of life. *It is in reality the fulfillment of life.* "He that loseth his life for my sake shall find it" (Matthew 10:39). That paradox from the lips of Jesus is ultimate wisdom.

One really begins to live, only when one loses oneself in God's purpose. When we escape from the blindness of selfishness into the perceptions of self-giving love; when the future is unknown and we commit ourselves to the wisdom of God; when our personal frailty is realized and we turn ourselves over to the God who is perfect beauty and truth and goodness; when we so despair of our inner contradictions and outer impotence that we abandon ourselves to the Creator, Redeemer, Sanctifier, to be dealt with as only creative, redeeming, sanctifying wisdom, love, and power can—then we find true life.

The humble person discovers that such abandonment loses nothing that is worth keeping but finds God with a quick vividness that is breathtaking and thrilling. When praying there are no more self-devised plans and purposes intruding themselves between self and God. Nor is the mind busied with dreams and demands rising out of a subtle egoism that assumes that it knows best.

The humble person wants God as the thirsty seeks water or the hungry seeks bread. God's will is desired as a sick person wants the will of the trusted physician. With the whole heart eagerly committing itself to God, such a person enters into a vivid awareness of the God who is always at hand, waiting to deal with human willingness, and the God who is available when human willingness has been cleansed and made ready by disciplines and by grace.

Humility is not weakness but strength, for it receives the strength of God. Humility is not folly but wisdom, for it is open to the ever available wisdom of God. Humility is not nothingness but fullness, for the fullness of God pours into the vacuum created by the demolition of human pride and self-sufficiency.

"Blessed are the poor in spirit: for theirs is the kingdom of heaven" (Matthew 5:3). "He that shall humble himself shall be exalted" (Matthew 23:12). "Humble yourselves therefore under the mighty hand of God, that he may exalt you in due time" (1 Peter 5:6).

The Disciplines Of Humility

Such humility is not easily attained. Only God is sufficient for the quest. The quest must really be a conquest—a conquest of the proud, assertive, self-sufficient, worldly-wise, managerial ego. The only power able for such a conquest is the God of our Lord Jesus Christ. In vain we struggle without Him. When victory comes we will know that it is *through* "him that loved us, and washed us from our sins in his own blood, and hath made us kings and priests unto God and his Father" (Revelations 1:5,6).

But here as elsewhere we have a role to play. God bestows humility only on those who practice humility. God gives victory over self only to those who are willing to accept the challenge of battle and make war on the self. "Humble yourselves" is the divine summons.

"He that humbleth himself," said Jesus, he it is whom God exalteth by victory. (See Luke 14:11.) Even of Christ, it is avowed, he "made himself of no reputation, and took upon him the form of a servant, and . . . humbled himself" (Philippians 2:7,8). Having thus portrayed the life of Jesus, we are likewise challenged to "let this mind be in you, which was also in Christ Jesus" (Philippians 2:5).

Below are some suggestions that will help you practice the discipline of humility. But do not assume that you, alone, by practicing them can achieve your own deliverance from your egocentric self. Such an assumption would only foster pride. That would be an anomaly, wouldn't it—to become proud of your progress in humility! So use these disciplines faithfully, but also in dependence on God.

1. *Begin the day by looking at Jesus.*

Nothing is quite so humbling as even a cursory glance at His perfections. Self-satisfaction disappears when one watches Him moving up and down the roads and streets of Galilee and Jerusalem.

Take time to read from the gospels the story of something Jesus did or said, and contrast it with what you do or say.

If there is no opportunity to read, then recall some episode in His life or some phrase from His teachings, and set your own life and words in that light.

2. *Recall your own sins and imperfections.*

Do not do it morbidly, but do it realistically. Say to yourself, "That is the kind of person I am." Such recognition is wholesome medicine for the sickness of complacency.

3. *Forget the imperfections of others.*

To dote on the sins of others is to foster pride. Remember the Pharisee: "God, I thank thee, that I am not as other men are" (Luke 18:11). A contemporary said to his friend, "When I look at others, I conclude that I am not so bad after all." Along that way lies moral and spiritual death, so check yourself anytime you find your mind dwelling on the faults of your neighbors.

4. *Beware of seeking honor from others.*

Endeavor to keep out of the "limelight." In public assemblies be inconspicuous. Stay away from the platform. Recall the counsel of Jesus, "When thou art bidden of any man to a wedding . . . go and sit down in the lowest place" (Luke 14:8-10). Deliberately spurn to seek office and recognition. Never "play to the galleries."

5. *Consider others better than yourself.*

Every day do something in the spirit of the apostle Paul's exhortation, "in honour preferring one another" (Romans 12:10). That will hurt, but it will hurt where you need to be hurt—in your pride.

6. *Learn the joy of giving and serving anonymously.*

When you do a good deed, make a contribution, send flowers to the sick or bread to the hungry, do it in the name of Christ only! "Let not thy left hand know what thy right hand doeth" (Matthew 6:3).

7. *Avoid the trap of self-exaltation.*

Resist all temptation to "set yourself up" in the eyes of other people. "In humility count others better than yourselves" (Philippians 2:3 *RSV).*

8. *Each day find something to do that is considered beneath your station.*

Remember Jesus who "rose from supper, laid aside his garments and girded himself with a towel

. . . and began to wash the disciples' feet" (John 13:4,5 *RSV*). Do the job around the home or in the office or at the church that nobody else wants to do.

9. *Never make an effort to be seen in the company of important people.*

"Associate with the lowly" (Romans 12:16 *RSV*). Go and sit by the person whom others avoid. Even Jesus scorned the company of Pharisees to be with publicans and sinners.

10. *Learn to recognize virtue in everyone.*

Curb your tongue the moment it begins to find fault with others. Fault-finding is a manifestation of the ego at its worst. "Who art thou that judgest another?" (James 4:12).

11. *Cultivate a cheerful heart.*

Remember that "godliness with contentment is great gain" (1 Timothy 6:6). Eliminate any disposition to complain about your situation. Such complaint implies that you deserve something better. You don't! None of us does. Tell your ego that!

12. *Exercise humility of mind.*

Restrain your inclination to give advice to everyone. Advice is cheap and makes the poor assumption of having superior knowledge.

13. *Limit your speech-making.*

"Much and willing speaking is the effect of self-love and pride; for commonly it flows from an opinion that we can speak well, and consequently out of a desire of gaining estimation from others. . . . But such intentions and designs as these, the disciple of true humility and spirituality will abhor" (*Holy Wisdom,* p. 236).

14. *Cheerfully accept humiliations.*

"We desire to be humble but we want to pick and choose the means of becoming so for ourselves, which only means that our supposed humility is nothing else but self in a new disguise. The only pure way of becoming humble is the training of ourselves to say, 'Deo gratias' (thanks to God), for the daily inconveniences, difficulties, slights, unpleasant tasks, imperfections, failures, reproofs, etc., the acceptance of all those things which 'go against the grain'." (*The Art of Mental Prayer,* p. 182).

15. *Finally, take time for prayer.*

Teresa was right when she wrote, "Humility is the principal aid to prayer," but the converse is equally true. Prayer is the principal aid to humility when that prayer is "loving attention to God." Through such prayer, the finite self sees itself in the light of the infinite Self. It is convinced of its own nothingness in comparison with "the fullness of God"; its own ignorance in comparison with the divine wisdom; its own sinfulness in comparison with the divine holiness; its own selfishness in comparison with the divine love.

In that vision of divine perfection, no self-importance can survive; nor is there left any vestige of self-will.

Scripture Readings For The Week:

Sunday: Humility: God's requirement.
Micah 6:6-8

Monday: Christ's exhortation to be humble.
Luke 14:7-11

Tuesday: The open door for God.
James 4:6-10

Wednesday: Putting on humility.
Colossians 3:12-14

Thursday: The blessedness of humility.
Matthew 5:1-9

Friday: The secret to rest of soul.
Matthew 11:25-29

Saturday: Examples of humility.
Matthew 3:11,12; 8:5-8

Frugality

7

Frugality

Frugality is a word scarcely more acceptable to the average American than humility.

Once in a while we do discern some values in the humble life. But when have we been ready to praise frugality? We are more likely to scorn frugality as stinginess and penny-pinching. We pity miserliness.

We are disciples of the abundant life. So was Jesus! But we identify the abundant life with the multiplication of things—with money to buy and products to be bought. Jesus never did that. He saw trouble ahead for everyone who "fared sumptuously every day" (Luke 16:19).

Frugality: Economic Absurdity?

We talk much of the economy of abundance, which usually means bumper crops, roaring factories, swift assembly lines, huge production; goods and more goods for everybody; universal employment for people who in turn become universal buyers of an ever-increasing variety of products for ever-larger houses and more expensive wardrobes and more heavily laden dinner tables.

If factories are to run continuously, there must be an expanding market for goods. That means increased spending on the part of millions. So any talk about frugality seems not only an economic absurdity but an assault upon those high standards of living that we consider synonymous with human welfare.

Frugality was recently presented to a group of distinguished leaders who were considering the disciplines of the deeper life. They had accepted without question such other disciplines as obedience, humility, charity, purity. But at the mention of frugality they demurred vigorously. They believed that wide practice of it would upset our economy and inflict hardship upon a multitude of people. They believed that we must spend our way to universal prosperity—and that any serious limitation of spending meant idle factories, unemployment, and poverty.

This is not the place to discuss economic questions. It must be said, however, that there is something terribly wrong with an economy that can conceive of society only in terms of policies that undermine human character. If we can have economic prosperity only at the price of moral and spiritual frustration, then this is a crazy world. It contains in itself an inherent contradiction. More likely, it is not the nature of things that is absurd, but we who are off-balance. Maybe if we were wiser, we could conceive of an economic order that provided for the material necessities of life without endangering spiritual values and necessities.

At any rate, this chapter contends that frugality, in this or any social order, is an essential discipline for those who would enter into redemptive fellowship with God.

Materialism Vs. Asceticism

One of the tyrants, which dominate our lives and keep us from giving God our uninterrupted, intense, devoted attention, is *things*.

Things do play a necessary role in all our lives. We must have food and clothing and shelter; transportation, medicine, sanitation. "Refresh me with apples; for I am sick of love" (Song of Solomon 2:5). The most enraptured romantic eventually comes down to earth and to apples and all they symbolize. We are bodies as well as minds. Material bodies depend upon materials for sustenance.

We have five senses, whose action binds us to things—the eye to pleasant scenes; the ear to "the concord of sweet sounds;" the nose to fragrance; the touch to comfortable chairs and beds and temperatures; the tongue to delectable food. These same senses keep our minds and bodies vividly alive to all the material of existence. It is not strange that we have taken an adjective which the Bible reserves for God, *gracious,* and employed it to describe a mode of existence characterized by an abundance of things—"gracious living."

In most religions there are people who have affected a contempt for things. We call them "ascetics." That is hardly the correct word, however. It comes from a Greek word "askein," and means "to practice in a gymnasium." Even one who practices in a gymnasium must eat and wear clothes—and have a gymnasium to practice in! The gymnast is not a "thing-despiser," but rather a "thing-master," using things for the fulfillment of a purpose. The gymnast uses things that will contribute to the excellence and the victory that are sought. The gymnast is an athlete!

Frugality does not point toward asceticism, but "athleticism," as Gerald Heard calls it. Frugality is the mastery of things for chosen ends.

Why Frugality?

Frugality, properly understood and practiced, is one way to shake us free from the tyranny of things. It is what that modern saint, Evelyn Underhill, meant when she wrote to a friend: "What has to be cured is desiring and hanging onto things for their own sake!"

It is not difficult to understand how frugality helps in such a cure. When one merely eats and drinks and acquires by impulse—or even if one asks intelligent questions as to values or ability to pay—one is under the dominion of things. By rationalizing that dominion, one is persuaded that self, family, health, or the neighborhood will be the better for the purchase. But in reality, one buys because one cannot say no to a thing that is desired. A buying habit is set up that becomes tyranny.

The same tyranny that rules one in the store also rules one at the altar. What you are at prayer is what you are outside prayer. What dominates your thinking on the street or in the store will dominate it when you are kneeling. When you direct your mind toward God, you will be thinking of things, desiring things, fearing the loss of things, and scheming to acquire things. If God is thought of at all, you may try to make God your agent in the acquisition of things, so that you never have real fellowship with God.

But if frugality is practiced, which means you say no to things for thing's sake, and yes to things only when some higher values require the presence of things, you will be setting up a thought pattern that will increasingly be independent of things. Again, but in reverse, *what you are free from in the store, you will be free from at the altar.* When you try to direct your mind away from things to God, you can do it, because you have earned an independence from things that frees you from their tyranny.

Developing A Healthy Independence

Frugality is also important in relation to people. If one is to turn the attention from people to God and to be absorbed in God, it will be because one has developed an independence of people.

One type of neurotic is the person who cannot get along without people—one who is dependent on them for approval and affection. Approval helps us all, and we are certainly unfortunate if no one bestows upon us the blessing of genuine affection. Approval and affection are values unless and until we have to have them. Then they become tyrants.

In my long years as pastor-counselor, I have encountered many people who have "loved not wisely, but too well." Sometimes they have been youths faced with pre-marital paternity. Sometimes it has been a husband or wife involved in extra-marital entanglements. Seldom has it been sheer lust of the flesh, but rather people who were hungry for affection and sought it where it was to be found. If they had been independent of the need for affection, their tragedy never would have happened.

Many others haven't gone so far, but they're still dependent on people. They cannot stand alone, and thus, they never are alone—even in prayer.

They have become so dependent on people that when they are seeking God's presence, they are pursued and dominated by people—the hungering for people, the fear of losing people, the plans for corralling desirable people in their circle.

Here again, Evelyn Underhill writes so wisely about a friend: "Tell her it is all right to love people all she can, *so long as she loves with and in God and does not clutch at them.*"

By the practice of frugality in personal relationships, one develops a mental attitude that helps toward independence. That is a sound law of friendship: "One is only fit for friendship who can get along without it." That is also a biblical truth: "He that loveth father or mother more than me is not worthy of me" (Matthew 10:37). Christ's promise is to "every one that hath forsaken houses, or brethren, or sisters, or father, or mother . . . for my name's sake" (Matthew 19:29).

What we are proposing here is not life-negation. It is life-affirmation, but on a higher level than things or even people—on the divine level. Frugality as to things and people will prove to be the key to the abundance of God in which even things and surely people will fulfill their divine function.

Let us finish the quotation from Matthew: "Every one that hath forsaken houses, or brethren, or sisters, or father, or mother, or wife, or children, or lands, for my name's sake, shall receive an hundredfold, and shall inherit everlasting life" (Matthew 19:29).

We lose everything to find God. Then we find not only God, but everything is heightened in significance and sanctified. Frugality in things means that the remaining things become a sacrament. Frugality in personal relationships means that all people become dear to us for God's sake.

The Disciplines Of Frugality

While these do not pretend to be a complete schedule of helpful practices, they are suggestions born out of the rich experience of great souls in all ages. They are not to be made legalistic injunctions. Rather they should be regarded as friendly aids toward the quest in which we are engaged.

1. *Begin with food.*

As Cassian said once: "There can be no virtue till a soul has come to some mastery here."

—Let health, not appetite, be the measure of your eating.

—Do not pamper yourself with expensive gourmet delicacies. They are not necessary to health. Their use is simply indulgence. You are learning frugality.

—Avoid eating between meals. Learn to say no to friends who insist on your joining them for food and drink.

—Practice fasting regularly. It is a dietetically sound procedure that gives you a chance to say no. Of some appetites, as well as other demons,

94

it is true as Jesus said: "This kind can come forth by nothing, but by prayer and fasting" (Mark 9:29).

2. *Frugality in sleeping is important.*

—Rise an hour before the rest of the family. While body and mind are rested, you will have a wonderful opportunity to hold communion with God. Moreover, you will find conquering sleep another effective way of emancipating your life from the tyranny of the flesh. The saints have always been early risers.

—A full stomach makes for sluggishness of spirit. That we know. The glutton is never conspicuous for godliness. But I wonder if we have considered the fact succinctly expressed in *Holy Wisdom* ? "A full repast doth not so much . . . dispose her (the soul) for spiritual exercises, as for a long and profound sleep" (page 271).

—Those who would be free to commune with God must conquer both plate and pillow.

3. *Frugality, in all the expressions and satisfactions of the physical nature, is demanded.*

—The marriage relation should not be one of unbounded license.

—Here, where body and spirit unite in the mutual self-giving, which in true love is a sacrament of the deeper union that is the goal of every marriage, the battle for sainthood may be won or lost.

—Here, unless mutual self-giving alternates with mutual withholding, not only are the deeper meanings of the experience lost, but the richest experience of God becomes impossible. The sacrament will degenerate into a mere relief of organic tensions. Relief will become a habit. And habit, enslaving the mind, will make impossible a free and intensive attention to God.

Do not defer or deny this strategy!

4. *Avoid buying things even when you can afford to.* Make it a business to turn away from the counters where tempting goods are displayed.

—Ask yourself, "Do I really need this?" Do not let your desires cloak themselves in the disguise of necessity. Many things you can buy, you do not need—so don't!

—Try to return from the market or bargain sale each time *without* some goods you really wanted!

5. *Practice frugality in your personal relationships!*

That does not mean denial of fellowship, nor does it imply a quenching of affection. God forbid!

—Frugality implies a certain detachment, meaning you will cherish them but not cling to them; you will love them as God loves them—not for your own sake but for their sake. You will be their benefactor and not their slave. Frugality means you can get along without them if death or alienation comes.

They must not come between you and God, and they must not distract your attention from God. This new tranquility in your friendship and love will not make it a "crush" but a benediction!

—There is a withholding that is a true giving.

—There is a restraint that has real benefit.

—There is a frugality that is salvation for them and for you!

6. *Practice frugality in all your relationships.*

—Serve wherever you can but do not meddle in things that do not belong to you and in which you have no competence.

—"Whatsoever thy hand findeth to do, do it with thy might" (Ecclesiastes 9:10). Do not become so emotionally involved in each task that failure will bring despondency, or success elation and pride.

—Be friendly with all whom you encounter, but do not engage in unnecessary conversation and prolonged visits. The tongue can become a snare from which pilgrim's feet find escape difficult.

—Be ready always to receive the truth but do not indulge in a mere curiosity for information about various matters. One's mind can be under the tyranny of trash when one tries to get to God—and it is a vexing slavery. Have you never found drivel invading your prayer hour—some silly witticism, some parody on a prayer or hymn?

—Avoid the curiosity that will taint the mind with similar trash. "Finally, brethren, whatsoever things are true, whatsoever things are honest, whatsoever things are just, whatsoever things are pure, whatsoever things are lovely, whatsoever things are of good report; if there be any virtue, and if there be any praise, think on these things" (Philippians 4:8).

Scripture Readings For The Week

Sunday: Frugality in the common life.
Luke 3:10-14

Monday: Blessings of frugality.
Luke 6:20-25

Tuesday: Frugality in practice.
Luke 10:1-7

Wednesday: Frugality vs. covetousness.
Luke 12:13-21

Thursday: Frugality vs. anxiety.
Luke 12:22-31

Friday: Frugality in the use of money.
Luke 16:10-15

Saturday: The frugality of Jesus.
Luke 9:51-62

Generosity

8

Generosity

"*Generosity*—one of the essential disciplines? Now you're talking! You won't have to argue with me there. I always felt that there was something splendid about a generous person. God must like that person, too!"

That is the normal reaction to the theme of this chapter. The stingy person is no friend of ours. We do not see how such a one could be God's friend. We apply hard names such as "skin-flint," "tightwad," and "miser." We avoid the stingy person and cannot believe God wants such company either.

On the other hand, philanthropists evoke our admiration. We praise them while they live and build monuments in their honor after they die. Generous citizens, however small their resources, are beloved citizens. When we hear of their gifts and services we are proud to call them friends.

The tender heart and bountiful hand captivates us all. Eugene Debs was hated by many because of his social theories. But few who hated him could maintain their hatred when they heard that one wintry day he gave his own overcoat to a man who appealed for help.

A preacher stood by an open grave, reciting the last rites for a member of his parish. The bitter weather and icy wind pitilessly penetrated even the warmest garments. The preacher was shivering and heroically trying to keep his teeth from chattering during the committal service and the final prayer. He wore no overcoat—a pathetic contrast to the heavily clad folk who were gathered about the grave. The woman who wrote me about it said, "I knew what had happened without asking. He had given his overcoat to someone else. He was *that* kind of man!" You and I easily believe that kind of man or woman is God's kind.

Generosity Vs. Possessiveness

In the struggle to free ourselves for fellowship with God, I wonder if we realize the significance of generosity. This is not merely a trait that pleases God but a practice that releases humanity from bondages to the ego and to things.

The ego is strongly possessive. Its possessiveness is revealed in all its relationships. Left to itself, the ego is persistent in acquiring and in keeping. Sharing is not one of its passions.

The ego is possessive of things and has to be taught to give. Often self gives only under compulsion or because giving is good for business or social advancement. Even under the influence of religion we tithe, often on the assurance that God prospers the tither and makes the remaining nine-tenths go farther than the ten-tenths would otherwise stretch. That, of course, is not giving but trading. Far from being generous the ego is striking a good bargain by taking out social insurance with the Celestial Casualty Company.

Giving is not a trait of the ego—owning is! "Mine" is its dearest adjective. "Keep" is its most beloved verb!

The ego is possessive. Its possessiveness in property manifests itself as stinginess, miserliness, and greed. All these are rationalized as thrift, economy, good management, "saving for a rainy day," and "looking out for number one."

Possessiveness of people makes jealous friends, husbands, wives, and parents. That jealousy is rationalized as love, devotion, and loyalty.

Most persons who are possessive never recognize its hold on their lives. So complete is the domination of the ego that it is unconscious. Possessiveness just seems natural, and it is natural, being characteristic of our perverted egocentric nature. Possessiveness, however, is actually foreign to the new nature God intended us to have by God's grace.

Because of this possessiveness of the ego, the practice of generosity significantly contributes to the denial and repudiation of the self. Faithfully practiced, generosity undermines the ego. Every defiance of the ego's tyranny weakens its authority, so to speak. Every departure from the pattern it sets makes the next variation easier. We are made that way.

Our mind easily falls into patterns, which we call habits. Capable of a wide variety of patterns, our mind can be habitually willful or obedient, artful or simple, proud or humble, extravagant or frugal, miserly or generous, egocentric or we-centric or God-centric. The task of changing the patterns is partially our responsibility. Renewing the mind is possible by fixed purpose, consistent practice, and prayer that transforms us into the divine nature.

Poverty For Some, Generosity For All

All saintly people have undertaken the disciplines of generosity, and there is no place where their lives bear a clearer witness.

Some have assumed the vows of poverty. Antoinette said that even one penny was enough to keep her from God. Some have felt a necessity "to get rid of the verb, to *have,* in all its moods and tenses."

St. Francis and his "troubadours of God" renounced all worldly possessions.

Evelyn Underhill writes in her testimony: "The saints I have known in the flesh have often been quite unable to keep anything for themselves."

Obviously, all of us cannot do that. A dear friend of ours, burdened with the management of property and administration of estates, said one day in her weariness: "I have almost come to the place where I feel 'blessed be nothing'!" But there has to be "something," and some of us have to be responsible for providing and managing that "something."

The vow of poverty can never be more than the consecration of the few who are supported by the quite different labors and consecration of the many. Poverty is a vocation for some. In society as it is now organized, property is the vocation of others.

Each vocation has its peculiar liabilities and temptations that can be managed only by appropriate disciplines. The vocation of property, small or great, especially requires the discipline of generosity.

Giving All To God

It is important that generosity be generous! Much so-called generosity is really only a farce. It has none of the qualities of the truly generous spirit.

Here I give my all to Thee—
Friends, and time, and earthly store;
Soul and body Thine to be,
Wholly Thine forevermore!

Real generosity begins by giving everything to God! Everything means everything—not just a fraction, a tenth, a fifth, a half, but all.

Teresa, that blessed saint of long ago, said something that is as true of us as it was of dwellers in her era: "We think we are giving all to God, but in reality we are offering only the rent!"

Pere Rigoluec adds his own confession: "We pass years and sometimes all our life, hesitating as to whether we shall give ourselves entirely to God. . . . We reserve to ourselves many affections, desires, plans, hopes, pretensions."

Entire consecration is all too rare. We sing it often, but we do not live it. God has so little from us who are urged to love Him with all our heart, soul, mind, and strength that it is almost a parody to use the word "love" at all in describing our attitude toward the Creator.

Generosity is first giving ourselves to God wholly and finally, without reservation and without any lurking intent to take ourselves back again when it suits us or when conditions change. That kind of generosity toward God makes real generosity toward humanity easy if not inevitable.

Once what we are and have belongs to God, then the disposal of it rests with God. We are no longer owners but stewards. As God's managers, we await the divine word about the use of everything. It is amazingly simple after that! So simple, in fact, that until one yields all to God, it seems incredible!

Our disciplines should be making their way toward that kind of generosity with God. Sharing with God at any time moves us toward the final, complete surrender. When the goal of surrendering to God is kept constantly in mind, we will find it taking possession of our thoughts, growing upon us as possible and desirable. Much sooner than we anticipate we will arrive at the state of mind when we can say to ourselves: "How foolish this half-and-half living—partly my own, partly God's! Why not end it all now? Why not give myself and all that is mine to be God's forever?"

Where Does Generosity Begin?

Real generosity toward humanity is seldom practiced. We all give something of ourselves and our substance—sometimes directly, sometimes via the church, the Red Cross, and other religious and social service agencies. Our giving, however, lacks the liberality, bounty, and lavishness that generosity implies.

The newspapers once urged us to skip one meal a week and give the equivalent to the famine-stricken millions in Europe and Asia. One meal a week! When we have twenty other ample meals whose abundance will quickly restore the calories of the one missed meal!

I know one man who proposed to his wife that they send for relief the equivalent of *every* meal they ate. That was a little more like it, but even that was scarcely generous because they still would eat as usual. Their sacrifice, if any, would be the donation of funds that they would have devoted to other personal uses.

Generosity begins only at the point of sacrifice. Generosity does not give what we will never miss; to spare what will not make our own living more spare; to bestow on others what we ourselves can never use. That is true whether we are giving money, time, energy, counsel, or our very selves.

If we are seeking to undermine the ego, the bolder our strokes, the quicker the job will be done. Timid calculating gifts will scarcely affect our egocentricity. Only costly and consistent devotion to others of what we have and are frees us from the dominion of the ego, and sets us free to fellowship with both God and humanity.

Without generosity, frugality can easily degenerate into selfishness. A miser's refusal to spend may be motivated by a desire to accumulate all for self! By denying self and then devoting to others the money or energy or time saved, we will find ourselves making progress toward spiritual freedom.

The Disciplines of Generosity

1. *Begin now to give yourself to God.*
—Begin anywhere—with your next ten minutes or with the money in your pocket. Give that to God and ask what you should do with it.
2. *Renew your consecration during the day.*

—When you have time at your disposal, let it be God's time. Give God a chance to direct your use of it.

—When you are about to spend some money, stop and say: "Lord, this is really Yours. I want to act like it belongs to You. Shall I spend it or send it?"

—When you are thrown into the company of another, recognize yourself as God's agent. Give God your mind, your heart, and your tongue for that interview or conversation.

—When you sit down to read, give God the opportunity to direct your reading.

—When you make a plan or enter a transaction, lift your heart to God in prayer: "Lord, I am Yours. Let this business be Yours and not mine. You make the decisions now."

—When you have a free evening or a holiday, turn it over to the Lord, promising to go wherever God wants you to go and do whatever God wants you to do.

3. *Daily examine the management of your life.*

—See how much of it is in your own hands and how little belongs to God. Deliberately set your will to give more to God than you have before. Do not stop until you have made up your mind at exactly what points this larger consecration will begin—with your income, your friendships, your use of leisure time, your expenditures, or your vocation. Vagueness is futility. Be definite, concrete, and real.

4. *Consider how much God has done for you.*

—Ponder how little you have done in return. Let divine mercy melt your heart. Then let that melted heart set some new patterns of generosity for you. "Freely ye have received, freely give" (Matthew 10:8).

5. *Consider giving a whole day of your time to God.*

—Spend the day in prayer and fasting. Let God lend you to new opportunities for service to others.

6. *Remember your stewardship of God's resources.*

—Place all your money, property, and possessions at God's disposal without restricting the transfer of ownership. Should God decide to disperse those material goods, cooperate as the local agent for heavenly transactions.

7. *Make the matter of entire consecration a subject of frequent meditation.*

—Give yourself to God and renew the gift over and over until it becomes a reality.

Let us be true to the reckoning
And He will make it real.

8. *Each day give to someone something whose giving involves genuine sacrifice.*

—Set aside some time that you can scarcely spare and use it to give something of yourself, by letter, conversation, or deed to someone for whom you have no particular liking.

9. *Each day do something for someone who has no real claim upon you and can never repay you.*

—Occasionally remember the waiters and bellboys and room maids with a tip that will make them really happy. "If you do good to those who do good to you, what credit is that to you?" (Luke 6:33 *RSV*).

10. *The next time you subscribe to a worthy cause go "all out" for it.*

—Surprise your friends and yourself by true generosity. Be faithful to the task and committed to its completion. Be alert to "go beyond the call of duty" in having, giving, serving, and loving. "He which soweth bountifully shall reap also bountifully" (2 Corinthians 9:6).

Scripture Readings For The Week

Sunday:	Generosity toward the needy. *Matthew 5:39-42*
Monday:	Generosity of the spiritual treasure. *Acts 3:1-10*
Tuesday:	Giving everything to God. *Matthew 19:16-30*
Wednesday:	Generosity for employees. *Matthew 20:1-15*

Thursday: Cheerful giving.
2 Corinthians 9:6-15

Friday: Generosity vs. judgment.
Matthew 7:1-5

Saturday: God's giving.
Romans 6:23;
2 Corinthians 1:11;
9:15; Ephesians 2:8;
James 1:17

Truthfulness

9
Truthfulness

There has been much debate about the necessity of truthfulness. It usually is provoked by the simple, practical question, "Is a lie ever justifiable?" Only where life itself is at stake is the answer in the affirmative.

The Case For The Justifiable Lie

In serious illness, some physicians may argue that it is right to lie to the patient about his or her condition. They fear that the truth will literally frighten the patient to death. During wartime, nobody hesitates to lie to ruthless invaders about one's identity, feelings, or actions. In past wars, the underground or guerilla force has been one gigantic but subtle lie. If members told the truth, their lives would have been at stake.

It is interesting, however, to listen when thoughtful persons justify such behavior. They do not neatly dismiss the moral problem involved by simply asking, "What is a lie when a life is at stake?" Rather they claim that such lies are really the truth.

This is what they mean. In the case of critical illness, one seldom knows enough to say, "There is no hope." As long as there is life there is hope. Nature has amazing recuperative powers.

To say to an anxious patient, "You are seriously ill. You have one chance in a hundred," may convey not even that one chance exists. In a weakened state of mind the patient may interpret your words as a warning of inevitable death. You can communicate the real situation only by being unspecific. In order to say that the patient may yet recover, you employ an overstatement, such as that he or she is doing nicely.

To tell the truth in *any* situation, one must be certain that the hearer catches from one's language the idea in one's own mind. In this case the idea in the physician's mind is, "You may live." The only way the troubled mind of the sick man is likely to catch the idea is from language full of hope rather than language that is an exact scientific description of the real condition. Such is the argument.

In the case of underground warfare, it may likewise be argued that the activities and affirmations, though an apparent lie, are really part of a larger truth. To the enemy, those people are disloyal.

The case for the justifiable lie has been hastily sketched, showing how its supporters are paying a great tribute to truth. After all, what seems to be a lie in such situations is really the truth! The case for truth is impregnable, when even pleas for the justifiable lie justify the lie because it tells the actual truth!

One wonders if there could be any substantial argument about truthfulness being a valuable discipline to the spiritual life.

The Schemes Of The Ego

Most of the time the falsehoods that appear in speech and action are the efforts of the ego to secure or maintain some prize.

The ego wants pleasure. Often that pleasure is not available in socially approved form. The ego wants approval, too, so it must find a way to satisfy its desire for pleasure without frustrating its desire for approval. Self resorts to living a "double life" or secretly has "an affair".

The ego wants honors, but aware that such honors would not be given on the basis of real merit, it cheats on examinations. Self falsifies its own accomplishments, takes credit for the achievements of others, and "boosts" statistics. Even preachers fall prey to exaggeration in describing the size of their congregations. Self can be quite eloquent in telling "tall tales" of the battlefield, the trout stream, or the golf course.

The ego wants possessions, so it "drives sharp bargains" and "cuts the corners" on contracts,

117

making a larger profit than would be possible if the terms of the contract had been fulfilled. The ego falsifies the merits of its products.

One man made $15,000,000 selling a dandruff cure that did not cure. The government finally compelled him to discontinue the advertising that lied both about your dandruff and his patent medicine. But the $15,000,000 are still in his bank account, not in the pockets of those whom he defrauded!

Time would fail to tell of the books and the pictures, the cosmetics and the clothes, the food and the utensils, the "talent" and the services out of which other millions of dollars have been accumulated by deceiving the public. Wherever the informed see the words "colossal," "stupendous," and "gigantic," they know that they are in the presence of a lie told for the sake of a profit. Unfortunately, the multitudes do not know, and so the lie continues to be profitable.

The lie is the ego's cunning strategy for getting what it wants and keeping what it gets. For that reason, truth is one of the most effective strategies for the person who really wants to deflate and destroy the ego, thus removing hindrances to fellowship with God.

Philanderers, Climbers, and Tycoons

The ego lives by the satisfaction of its desires. "It grows by what it feeds upon." The man who secretly satisfies his passion for what he falsely calls "love" is at the same time inflating his ego. The woman who by deception gains honors, also acquires an increment of her ego. The man or woman who by fraud amasses wealth, also developes a massive ego.

Did you ever know a philanderer or a "social climber" or a "tycoon" who was not a superlative egoist? Philanderers do not know what love really is. They really love only themselves, hence, jealousies, quarrels, refined cruelties, and murders spring from their inflated egos.

The "climber," who may be busy in a multitude of social activities, is never a truly social person. The "socialite" is the most unsocial of beings, whose parties do not make him or her a real party to the welfare of others. Benefits are really for the benefit of the socialite's own ambitions.

Tycoons may be typhoons of egocentric schemes that destroy everything in their paths. Tycoons may promote the interests of others for their own benefits, but they cannot be wholly ruthless and prosper. Whatever contributions they make to the welfare of others, their major concern is with themselves.

Just as surely as the ego "grows by what it feeds upon," it loses power as it is denied. One way of denial is by truthfulness.

The person who decides to be truthful will cease philandering. There is no truth while having an affair. The philanderer lies about where he or she is. Others will become involved in similar lies. Only sheer truthfulness will end this indulgence.

One philanderer confessed to me: "I want to be respected. I know I would not be if people knew about all this. *I am going to be what I want people to think I am.*" Just the determination to be and act the truth brought that affair to an end. Truthfulness also curbed the ego's dominion, enabling other people and God to be included in its attention and interest.

The "social climber" who decides to be truthful finds it necessary to change a whole life-pattern; to cease the pretense of interest in others and develop a real interest; to quit "throwing parties" and to become a real party to movements that enhance the welfare of others. By changing patterns of behavior and thought, the dominion of the ego is lessened. This person is more at liberty to turn outward to others and to God.

The tycoon who decides to be truthful may still be a profit-seeker and an egocentric, but at least the ego has been denied the right to seek profit by falsehood. That denial is wholesome. Truthfulness is not the cure of selfishness, but it is a curb upon that narrow self-assertion that is wholly blind and ruthless.

We need truthfulness not merely to live in harmony with other human beings, but it is essential if we are to live with God in intimate fellowship.

By truthfulness we undermine the ego whose

tyranny deflects us from attention to and awareness of God. As the Bible insists, we become aware of God when we seek God with all our hearts. We cannot seek with all our hearts until our hearts are freed from dominant ego-concerns. Truthfulness is one way to help abolish such self-centeredness.

The Case Of The Tampered Scale

A word of caution is necessary here. Denis de Rougemant, in *The Devil's Share*, calls attention to the fact that there are two ways of lying. A merchant can charge a customer for a pound of sugar when the scale registers only fifteen ounces, or the scale can be tampered with so that fifteen ounces of sugar will register as a pound. Thereafter the merchant may say truthfully that the scale shows a pound, though only fifteen ounces are there. Eventually, the merchant forgets all about the tampered scales and may even add a few spoonfuls for good measure and feel good about it. Nevertheless, the weight is still a lie.

There are many ways of "tampering with the scale": by corrupting a word until it no longer registers the meaning it is supposed to register; by a false emphasis in a sentence, so that the emphasis belies what the sentence would say if left alone; by a gesture that denies the explicit meaning of the language accompanying it.

You may recall the political candidate who

found himself confronted by babies whom he kissed for a vote's sake, but whom he could not truthfully praise as beautiful or bright. This politician sought a formula that would let him appear to approve of the babies, thus ingratiating himself with the parents, and yet be truthful.

Whenever a baby was thrust into his arms, the candidate would gaze at it with affected admiration and say, "Well, this is a baby." That was true—it was a baby and not a baboon or a buggy. But when he said, "This is a baby," the emphasis implied what he did not mean, that it was an unusually perfect specimen of an infant. So his truth was a lie. He had "tampered with the scales!" He had as effectively and unscrupulously supported the ego in its quest for power, as if he had said, "This is a beautiful baby," even though it had a face only a mother could love.

Truthfulness that is a discipline must be real truth telling. Otherwise the ego is not only confirmed in its sway but that sway is intensified because it *seems* to have the blessing of truth. A false self-righteousness further inflates the ego.

The Disciplines of Truth

1. Watch your words.
Ask yourself if you are saying exactly what you mean. Eliminate exaggerations. Ask yourself if your listener will receive as exact a picture of the

situation as you can give. Avoid misleading coloration of speech. Recall Aldous Huxley's warning: There is "a rhetoric which is tolerably true to facts as well as emotionally moving, and rhetoric which is unconsciously or deliberately a lie."

2. *Watch your tones.*

Inflections are often more misleading than direct falsehood. They are so subtle as to enter and deflect a mind that would detect a lie if put into plain speech.

3. *Watch your actions.*

A shrug of the shoulder, a "poker face," starting off in one direction when your real destination is in another, a casual look, or a pose of intelligence may be just as untruthful as any falsity of speech.

4. *Study your associations.*

Ask yourself what you are seeking in your relations with people. Are your approaches genuine? Do you make people think you are doing what you do because you really like them or want to help them, when actually you like only yourself and merely want to use them?

5. *Searchingly appraise your calendar.*

Are your service and your activities the expression of a genuine desire to be a servant of your community, or is it a disguise under which your ego is seeking its own ends?

6. *Examine the impression you make.*

It is possible for one's whole life to be a lie; to create an impression that you believe one thing when you really believe something quite different; that you are one sort of person when you are just the opposite; that you seek one great goal when in fact your whole scheme of existence is a much lesser goal. What about that?

7. *Deal ruthlessly with hypocrisy.*

If you are not what words, tones, attitudes, and actions declare you to be, one of two courses can be followed: you can lower your words, tones, attitudes, and actions to the level of your present actual self; or you can by God's grace bring yourself up to the level of your words, tones, attitudes, and actions.

To do the former will not end the lie—for "all sin is a lie." It will only end the hypocrisy. To do the latter will not only end the lie but begin that socialization of the self, which in its perfection is the death of the ego. When we begin to be what we want people to think we are, the ego begins to lose its dominant place in life.

8. *Some simple but drastic disciplines:*

—Check your exaggerations, correct them, and apologize for them, no matter in whose company you are.

—Avoid plagiarism. In speech or in writing not claim as your own the idea or phraseology of another.

—Eliminate the urge to put on a "good front."

—When you find yourself striking a pose, abandon it at once.

—Quit singing things you do not mean, such as,

"I'll go where You want me to go, dear Lord."

—Stop all flattery—not sincere appreciation but flattery! You will be able to save two egos—your own and the other person's.

—Avoid indirections, subtlety, and "politics." If you cannot get what you want except by deceiving others as to your real intention, then go without. One of the most pious men I know always has "something up his sleeve." When he makes a proposal, his associates always ask, "What's he after now?" He would be hurt if you called him a liar, but that is what he is! You will be, too, if you act the same way. Quit it!

—Do nothing that you have to conceal. "Nothing is covered up that will not be revealed"(Luke 12:2 *RSV*).

—Stay away from the "whisperers." Secrecy is only another kind of falsehood. Eliminate it from your life.

You will be amazed to discover what a handicap absolute truthfulness will impose on the ego. Try it. At the end of a single day the proud, arrogant thing that set out in the morning with banners flying will come home at night like a bedraggled army, beaten and disgraced.

Scripture Readings for the Week:

Sunday: The tragedy of
              untruthfulness.
              Acts 5:1-11

Monday:	Truthfulness of speech. *Matthew 5:3-37*
Tuesday:	Truth and freedom. *John 8:31-34*
Wednesday:	Truth as armor. *Ephesians 6:13-20*
Thursday:	Truth in prayer. *Matthew 23:13-22*
Friday:	Inner truth. *Matthew 13:25-28*
Saturday:	Truthfulness of Jesus. *John 14:5-17*

Purity

10
Purity

Of course! Who could hope for fellowship with God if one is living an unchaste life?

Isn't it strange that when anyone begins to talk about purity, we so quickly assume that he is arguing merely for chastity? That is one meaning of the word, and in this adulterous generation it is an important meaning. When the concern for virginity is dismissed as superstition and promiscuity is condoned as necessity, it is time for us all to reaffirm that only "the pure in heart . . . shall see God" (Matthew 5:8).

We used to be troubled by those who advocated the double standard—purity for women, promiscuity for men. Nobody hears about the double standard any more, but not because men have become what women used to be. Today many women have joined the men in recognizing only one standard—impulse.

In the past, the threat of pre-marital maternity seemed to be the only real reason for abstention.

With the coming of effective contraceptives, however, there is no longer any need to refrain from following the impulse to its final satisfaction.

The purity that enables one to have fellowship with God, however, is still the chastity that refrains from extra-marital fellowships of the flesh.

The ego makes insistent claims in this area of sexual pleasure and is often intolerant of denials. It is here that it is subtle and inventive in its assertion of its needs. Unless the ego can be defeated in its usurpation of sex, it will remain a tyrant on the throne of one's entire life. Even when the physical capacity for fulfillment has vanished, in imagination and memory the ego will still manifest its terrible sway.

Not Merely A Matter Of Deed

Purity means vastly more than the absence of fleshly indulgence; it is a significant discipline of the abundant life. This larger meaning unfolds with the understanding that purity is not merely a matter of deed, but of intention—even a matter of imagination. "Whosoever looketh on a woman to lust after her hath committed adultery with her already in his heart" (Matthew 5:28).

Many have gone through life without an overt act of unchastity, yet have repeatedly committed the deed in imagination and desire. Impure imaginations and lustful desires, when fondly cherished, do something to the soul that is not beautiful to behold. The damage incurred later appears in perversions and abnormalities that afflict not only the one who lusts, but also innocent persons with whom he or she associates.

Desire is natural, but the person who is tempted can avoid cherishing such desires, lingering over them, fondling them, and imaginatively satisfying them in unlawful ways.

What Is Purity?

Purity, on which every teacher of religion insists, is not something that is related only to the sex phase of human experience. Lallemont calls purity "the primary means of attaining to perfection" and describes it as "not having in our heart anything the least contrary to God."

The justice of that description is evident to anyone who believes that we are made in the image of God. The Bible says, "We shall be like him; for we shall see him as he is" (1 John 3:2). If our original nature was to be like God, and restoring that likeness is God's greatest concern, then anything in us unlike God is an impurity.

Purity is freedom from anything foreign to the essential character of a thing. Pure water is water in which there is nothing but H_2O. Pure poetry is poetry that has nothing in it that is alien to the nature of poetry—no irregular verse, no lumbering prose, no arid didacticism. Pure science is science that has no extraneous or irrelevant interest but is concerned only in objective reality.

A pure person is one whose character is identical to God's intention for him or her. God planned that human beings would become partakers of the divine nature.

The Pursuit Of Purity

Who then can hope to be pure? Did you ever know anybody in whom there was absolutely nothing in the least contrary to God? Probaby not. Yet here at least is our goal. Jesus did not deal in relatives but in absolutes. He summoned us to the very perfections of God.

To aim at anything less is to have a lower aim for ourselves than Christ had for us. To argue about whether such purity is attainable is scarcely the business of most of us who have never made it our serious consecration, let alone our possession.

"Blessed are the pure in heart: for they shall see God" (Matthew 5:8). Instead of throwing up your hands in despair or decreasing your hunger for God in reversion to some lesser idol, seek purity. Seek it for ten years, for twenty years, for thirty. Then see what you think. People have been searching for values of vastly less significance for a longer period; some died searching.

Are we to refuse the challenge of the quest? Let me assure you that if you will make the purity of God your indefatigable quest, the God of purity will become yours in such fullness that your questions will be transcended in the splendor of the experience that has overtaken you.

Meister Eckhart said: "I shall never pray God to give me Himself. I shall pray God that He make me pure; for if I am pure, God must give Himself and dwell in me because it is His peculiar nature to do so."

Or, stating it in harmony with the thesis of this book: we will become aware of God when we are freed from the dominion of things, people, and the ego. Then we can fasten our attention on God and fulfill our purpose, which is to be aware not merely of lesser reality but of ultimate Reality.

Purity And The Other Disciplines

Let's consider purity in relation to the other disciplines—obedience, simplicity, humility, frugality, generosity, truthfulness. To be pure means all of these things. Purity means eliminating from our lives all self-will, all ostentation and artificiality, all pride, all indulgence, all miserliness, and all falsehood. Only then can we be obedient, simple, humble, frugal, generous, and truthful. Only then can we become like God.

Purity also means getting rid of everything that is unlovely or unloving, everything that is unjust, contentious, wrathful, uncharitable, resentful, fearful, snobbish, opinionated, prejudiced, arrogant, sluggish, short-sighted, sectional, sectarian, racist, fanatical, and unreal.

133

Purity also requires unmixed motives. "The single motive," says Grou, "is to please God and hence arises total indifference as to what others say and think, so that words and actions are perfectly simple and natural, as in His sight only."

The Disciplines of Purity

Let us remind ourselves that the purity we seek can never be our own achievement. There is a strange paradox here—only the pure in heart shall see God; only those who see God shall be pure in heart. No disciplines, none proposed here nor elsewhere, can make us pure.

It is equally true that without self-discipline there can be no divine deliverance. William Law has said it most effectively:

"They have no quickening or sanctifying power in them; their only worth consists in this, that they remove the impediments of holiness, break down that which stands between God and us, and make way for the quickening, sanctifying Spirit of God to operate on our souls, which operation of God is the one, only thing that can raise the Divine Life in the soul or help it to the smallest degree of real holiness or spiritual life."

1. To attain that lower purity, from the indulgence of the flesh:

—Read no books and see no movies that inflame desire. If the book you have innocently purchased is doing that, lay it aside; if a movie is the offender, get up and leave the theatre.

—Indulge in no stories nor listen to any that have an unclean reference to sex. Turn away from the company where these are the vogue. "Do not be deceived: 'Bad company ruins good morals' " (1 Corinthians 15:33 *RSV*).

—Avoid anything that lowers your inhibitions. How does smoking or drinking appear in the light of such a test?

—Set a watch at the door of your eyes. Lusting often begins with looking. Even Job said, "I have made a covenant with my eyes" (Job 31:1 *RSV*).

—Guard your imagination. In a contest between the will and imagination, the imagination usually wins. Your will to purity is unlikely to be able to cope with an imagination full of impure imagery. "Whatsoever things are pure"—let these fill your imagination (Philippians 4:8).

—Do not run into temptation. Some associations are very corrupting.

—Restrain your curiosity. That is especially important for youth. The fruit of the tree of the knowledge of good and evil has cost more than one youth his Eden.

—Let your thoughts dwell on what to do and be rather than on what to avoid and shun.

—Keep your mind occupied with Christ and the pattern He has given you.

2. To attain that higher purity, the freedom from all that is ungodly:

—Diligently cultivate purity of intention. Check yourself regularly to discover the love of gain, fame, or power mixed with the one motive to become like God.

—Do not follow those who are covetous and ambitious, or even respectable and who cloak their lust for power under the guise of idealism or politics. Rigidly watch for and crush the beginnings of such confusion of motives with the one motive, "Thy Kingdom come."

—Avoid any company, conversation, pictures, or reading that stimulates such ungodly ambitions in your mind or heart.

—Banish wayward thoughts that occupy the mind with the very things you seek to eliminate. Do not pasture your sheep just anywhere!

> *Her flocks are thoughts,*
> *She keeps them white,*
> *She guards them from the steep.*

—Read books and keep company with people who will fill your mind with noble aspirations, quicken your purpose, and strengthen your faith.

—Carry a "spiritual nosegay" with you. When visiting a garden, you gather a flower and let its beauty and fragrance sweeten your office or shop. So take away from your prayer or meditation some thought or purpose to sanctify the rest of the day.

—During the day, pause often, close your eyes, and let your mind rest upon God as revealed in

Jesus Christ—His purity, gentleness, strength, humility, and love.

—Practice Gertrude More's disciplines:

(1) Do all that any human or divine law demands of you.

(2) Refrain from doing anything forbidden by human or divine law or by special divine warnings.

(3) Bear with patience all contradictions, spiritual dryness, temptations, afflictions, loss of friends, lack of comforts or even necessities.

—Eliminate self-centered actions that have made you inconsiderate to your spouse, your children, and your friends.

—Curb self-interest, which makes you judge plans and policies by their effect on you, or people by their conformity to your taste, or God by God's affirmative answer to your clamorous desires.

—Practice that mortification described as the most difficult of all—a holy indifference to the success or failure of an enterprise to which you are giving everything you have and are. That is not being stoical or neutral. Become so devoted that you are not only willing but eager that God's will be done even though it means the defeat of what in all sincerity you have believed to be divine intent. That really is purity of heart—no desire that is not God's!

Scripture Readings For The Week

Sunday:	Purity at any price. *Matthew 5:27-32*
Monday:	The purity of God. *Matthew 5:43-48*
Tuesday:	Purity of intention. *Matthew 6:22-24*
Wednesday:	Purity of heart. *Matthew 15:8-20*
Thursday:	The purity of Jesus. *John 14:29-31*
Friday:	Self-purification. *John 3:1-3*
Saturday:	Purity of thought. *Philippians 4:4-9*

Charity

11
Charity

We have purposely changed the order of the disciplines as printed in the vows of the Disciplined Order of Christ and have reserved charity until last. Here is where charity belongs, for it is both the chief discipline and the consummation of all the other disciplines.

Where there is perfect charity there is perfection. The object of all our praying, striving, and disciplined living has then been attained. The ego's tyranny is finally overthrown. The self has turned completely to God and has union with God in a fellowship in which self finds its fulfillment. The prodigal has returned from wandering and taken off the rags of self-will. Clad in the robes of divine grace, the prodigal feasts at the Father's table, humbly accepting whatever place and task divine love appoints. At last it is known that, not in independence but "in His will, is our peace."

Why Not Love?

We have purposely retained the word *charity* instead of the word which the Revised Version uses—*love*.

The reason is simple: Love has become cheapened in value. It is not merely that we have overworked it—though we have done that. A continental visitor asked his host if Americans did not know anything to sing about but "love!" If you spend the evening watching TV or listening to the radio, you may share that European's wonder.

But the cheapening and vulgarizing of the word *love* has resulted not so much from its over-use as from its misuse. We have identified it with infatuation, passion, the piracy of someone else's wife or husband, promiscuity, romantic egoism, masochism, sentimental adventure, eroticism, neuroticism, domestic instability, prolonged infantilism, parental possessiveness, the Oedipus complex, obsession with a father or mother image, torments of jealousy, and seduction.

Was ever a word in our language so soiled and spoiled as this word, which in its highest meaning is what God is? The most sublime utterance in the Bible is a three-word clause at the end of a sentence in the first epistle of John: "God is love" (1 John 4:8). One is almost afraid to quote that text because of all the hideous ideas that our fantastic and furious living has associated with love.

The word *charity* also has its limitations for the same reason, but at least it is a clean word. We often make it mean merely giving to someone in poverty or need. But we never apply it to the hideous mockeries that in a multitude of minds have come to be associated with the word *love*. We have limited the significance of charity; not soiled it.

Charity Defined

What is charity? In the long history of the search for God, the answers to that question have a striking uniformity. It would be rash to turn a deaf ear to the great saints of Christendom and try to redefine this quality of spirit by which they lived and through which they entered into vivid fellowship with God. We bring you their witness.

1. *Charity is unselfishness.*

It seeks nothing for itself—not even God. It seeks God for God's sake. It asks for neither gift nor reward. Charity seeks people not for what it can get from them but for what it can give to them. It loves God for God's own sake. It loves people for God's sake. "Charity . . . seeketh not her own," said the apostle Paul (1 Corinthian 13:4,5).

"Some people want to see God with their eyes as they see a cow, and to love God as they love their cow—for the milk and cheese and profit it brings them. This is how it is with people who love God for the sake of outward wealth or comfort. They do not rightly love God, when they

143

love God for their own advantage. . . . Any object you have in your mind, however good, will be a barrier between you and the inmost Truth"—Meister Eckhart.

One of the distressing characteristics of our age is the many cults and movements that invite people to God because of what they can get. They try to use God as they use the experts they employ—their physician and lawyer and banker. Their interest in God parallels their interest in a garage when their automobile breaks down. They want help. They are willing to pay for it. They are no more eager to associate with God than with the mechanic. When trouble is past they forget God just as quickly as they forget the mechanic who fixed their car. Maybe they want God around but only as they want their chauffeur. They are afraid or unable to drive alone. Beyond the role of servant to their needs, they have no use for God.

Charity is just the antithesis of that. At its best charity wants nothing from God, except God. It is willing even to go without God, if that is to God's glory. Charity is being so in love with God that it gives itself totally to God, asking only the privilege of such selfless self-giving and rejoicing in it.

2. *Charity is not an emotion.*

All the saints are agreed upon that. Charity is an act of the will—a resolution and a determination born in a sense of value and renewed day after day. As Bede Frost says, charity is not a sentimental feeling, but "a constant act of the will, choosing God before anything else."

St. Teresa, one of the greatest of saints, with the relentless clarity that characterized her thinking and living, wrote, "Let everyone understand that real love of God does not consist in tearshedding, nor in that sweetness and tenderness for which we usually long, just because they console us, but in serving God in justice, fortitude of soul, and humility."

Father Baker adds his own testimony, always convincing to those who know the character of his life and work, "Charity . . . is a resolute determination of the superior will to seek God and a perfect union with Him; the which resolution she will not give over for any distractions or occurring difficulties whatsoever. . . . And such a resolution is grounded on a high esteem we have, by faith, of the infinite perfections of God and the innumerable obligations laid by Him on us."

We must remember this. One of the most common mistakes is the assumption that charity is a tender emotion, quite like the romantic feeling that overtakes a young man or woman in what we call "love at first sight."

If that were charity, then we might well despair at the exhortation to practice it. We just cannot make ourselves "feel" that way about everybody or even about God. Emotions are not to be commanded in that fashion. Ultimately there is great feeling in our relationship with God. We are often "lost in wonder, love, and praise." But at the beginning, no effort of our own can produce such rapture.

Furthermore it is spiritually unhealthy to seek a feeling. That is egoism of the worst sort, even though the feeling sought is love. The worshipers who go to church on Sunday in quest of a pleasant emotion are not really worshipers. They are narcissists and sometimes neurotics!

But with the understanding that charity is an act of the will, we move out of despair and neuroticism into a realm where religion makes sense. The discipline of charity becomes a mature Christian's method of achieving and receiving deliverance from egoism and entering into an awareness of God.

Surely, one can *will* to seek nothing for oneself, to ask no gifts and no rewards, to give self to God and to people for God's sake. The mere willing, in itself, cannot effect such a result. But the mere willing is our part. We can make such a resolution and practice it day after day.

If we cannot dictate emotions, we can form an intention. We know in every realm how an intention, followed and supported by right thoughts and right acts, grows stronger and more determined. How much more true is it of an intention that is in harmony with the divine will?

To the natural development of such an intention is added the cooperative and empowering grace of God, working within us "both to will and to do of his good pleasure" (Philippians 2:13). So the will to charity becomes the grace of charity. When that grace is complete, neither the ego, nor things, nor people have dominion over us. Only then can we turn wholly, simply, and irreversibly to God.

Then we will be in the real heaven. To quote Father Baker once more: "The difference between heaven and hell is that hell is full of nothing but self-love and propriety (proprietorship); whereas there is not the least degree of either in heaven."

The Disciplines Of Charity

1. *Showing charity toward humanity.*
—Never under any circumstances retaliate for an injury. Retaliation means that you are thinking in terms of the good you have been seeking from others (and they have failed to give you). Charity thinks in terms of what *you* can do for them.

—Avoid anger. When it arises, banish it quickly. You are developing or seeking to develop the spirit that loves others, not for the sake of their goodness but for God's sake.

—Forgive quickly when others seek pardon. That is not easy if they have done you great injury, but it is necessary. Nothing is a greater promoter of true charity than ready forgiveness.

—Forgive others before they ask it. The charity that "suffereth long, and is kind" (1 Corinthians 13:4) does not harbor resentments. Let your heart be like Lincoln's—"no room for the memory of a wrong"—and like Christ's, who, even while enemies were nailing him to a tree, not only forgave, but asked God to forgive them.

—Pray for others, good and bad, friend and foe, family as well as strangers.

—Do good to everyone you meet. Try not to let anyone come and go without receiving some bounty from your heart or hand.

> *Look all around you*
> *Find someone in need;*
> *Help somebody today.*

—Be courteous to all. Practice saying thank you and please.

—Rejoice at the success of others as quickly as you sorrow at their misfortune. Caring and sharing are greatly conducive to charity.

—Sacrifice for others. Do it anonymously. Each day do something sacrificial for someone without revealing your identity.

—Keep love for people uppermost in your life. If you find yourself loving riches or pleasures or power more, rigidly curb these rivals.

—Never make the faults of others the subject of your conversation. That will destroy more charity in ten minutes than you can acquire in a week of faithful discipline.

—When there is a choice between the welfare of a neighbor and the satisfaction of personal desire, give preference to the neighbor's welfare.

—As you meet people casually on the street or in the market, take them into your loving thought and prayerful concern. Breathe a prayer for them and bestow a smile in passing.

2. *Having charity toward God.*

—Meditate on God's perfections, beauty, truth, goodness, holiness, justice, mercy, and love.

—Dedicate yourself to the incarnation of those perfections in you. Do not merely admire them; seek them. Count everything else but a trifle in comparison.

—Repent of your failure to be like God. "Blessed are they that mourn" (Matthew 5:4).

—Keep alive in you the purpose to serve God under all circumstances and on all occasions.

—Welcome every pleasant and unpleasant experience that God's providence permits to come into your life. Make no exceptions here—the weather, the rude clerk, the disappointments, the afflictions. These are not Godsent but the result of the freedom given to humanity for God's final glory.

—Develop the habit of doing and being everything for God's sake; loving others because God loves them; doing your work well because God loves excellence; being patient under provocation because that pleases and honors God.

—Never seek for comfort or ease but only seek to please God.

—Imitate God as much as possible. "Be ye therefore followers of God, as dear children" (Ephesians 5:1).

—Serve God as effectively as you can but learn to rejoice when others serve more effectively. That will require real self-forgetfulness and devotion to Christ.

—Seek only such pleasures, honors, and privileges as are found in God. Then all your experiences will wed you more closely to Christ.

—Never be content with the degree of love you have for God but seek to love God more and more.

—Rejoice in God's commands as well as God's gifts, in God's disciplines as well as blessings, in God's deprivations as well as bestowals.

Transcend, in loving God, all thoughts of yourself, your happiness and prosperity, your security and health.

Scripture Readings For The Week

Sunday: The classical description of charity.
1 Corinthians 13

Monday: Charity toward the sinful.
John 8:1-11

Tuesday: Charity for the weak.
Romans 14:10-19

Wednesday:	Charity toward our brethren. *Romans 15:1-6*
Thursday:	The test of our relationship to God. *1 John 3:10-18*
Friday:	Charity as love. *1 John 4:7-12*
Saturday:	Charity as forgiveness. *Matthew 18:21-33*

Important Cautions

12

Important Cautions

Every one of these disciplines is important and can be very useful to one who earnestly seeks an immediate awareness of God and direct communion with God. However, every one of them can be misused.

Faithfully and wisely practiced, these disciplines will aid our emancipation from the tyrannies that enslave us. They will also expedite the enthronement of Christ at the very center of life.

When *things* are dislodged from the seat of power in our lives, and *people* no longer hypnotize us with their opinions and their scale of values, and *the ego* is dethroned, then Christ will have an opportunity to communicate with us and captivate us with His wisdom and love.

"Christ in you, the hope of glory" (Colossians 1:27). Christ is the hope of glory, the one possibility of the splendor that is so lacking in our lives. Christ is the only source of divine vitality that is life indeed.

"If ye abide in me and my words abide in you" (John 15:7)—that is the big "if" that stands between our barrenness and fruitful, redemptive prayer and service. When abiding in Christ, prayer becomes communion, and service becomes a sacrament. His abiding in us becomes the presence for which our spirits cry, the comradeship that sweetens all loneliness, the victory that banishes all fear, the medicine that heals our diseases, and the answer that resolves all tragedy.

Discipline, then discovery, then deliverance, then doxology. That is the strategy this book recommends and seeks to clarify.

Discipline can be misused. Therefore this chapter must bring to its readers some cautioning counsel.

The Danger Of Keeping Score

Never practice discipline for its own sake.
Discipline is only the means to an end; it is not the end in itself. It is the way to a vivid awareness of God and to creative communion with God. But it is not the goal, and if discipline is regarded as such, it begets a subtle pride that is the enemy of God.

William Law reminds us of an ever-present peril:

> They practice them (the disciplines) for their own sakes, as though good in themselves; they think them to be real

parts of holiness, and so rest in them and look no further, but grow full of self-esteem and self-admiration for their own progress. This makes them self-sufficient, morose, severe judges of all that fall short. . . . Thus their self-denials do only that which indulgences do for other people; they withstand and hinder the operation of God upon their own souls, and instead of being really self denials, they strengthen and keep up the kingdom of the self.

Aldous Huxley in *The Perennial Philosophy* also stresses the peril of making disciplines an end in themselves:

The Puritan may practice all the cardinal virtues—prudence, fortitude, temperance, chastity—and yet remain a thoroughly bad man; for in all too many cases these virtues of his are accompanied by and indeed are causally connected with the sins of pride, envy, chronic anger and an uncharitableness pushed sometimes to the level of actual cruelty . . . he has fancied himself holy because he is stoically austere. But stoical austerity is merely the exaltation of the more creditable side of the ego at the expense of the less creditable.

It is not difficult to see why this is so frequently the story.

If, for example, in practicing the discipline of frugality, a person eats only a sandwich at lunch, refuses food or drink between meals; denies oneself the usual, last-minute slumber in the morning; returns from a bargain sale without an item that was both wanted and affordable; maintains a degree of detachment in personal relations; restrains undue curiosity about one's neighbors' comings and goings; and, if he keeps score—five light lunches this week, four refusals of invitations to the snack bar, six morning naps cut short in order to have time for prayer, one bargain sale lure resisted, one denial of temptation to eavesdrop though "just dying to hear what they were whispering about"; and if, week by week, something like this goes on, there is likely to be an inflation instead of deflation of the ego.

One begins to feel proud, to compare oneself most favorably with others who eat three square meals a day, who never let an afternoon pass without a trip to the soda fountain, who sleep until the last minute, who patronize every bargain sale that comes to town whether or not they really need what is offered there, and who never miss the "low-down" on some fellow citizen. Our disciplined friend may even begin to feel like a saint, though the saint never keeps score, never unfavorably contrasts others with himself, never feels that his or her disciplines are noteworthy, and is never proud of what he or she is doing!

The True Test

Disciplines are neither an end in themselves nor the proof of sainthood. The question is never, "What's the score?" but, "What's the spiritual result?" If these disciplines make one more self-conscious, self-centered, and self-satisfied, there is something wrong. The fault is not with the disciplines but with the perversion of them.

If one practices the clarinet, not in order to be able to play in an orchestra but to run up a record of hours practiced; or if one arises at four in the morning, not to master a subject but to be able to boast of one's conquest over sleep; or if one spends eight hours a day at a canvas, not to paint a stirring picture but to impress others with one's persistence, it could not be more of an absurdity than the idea of discipline as an end in itself.

The results are the test in every case. In one concert a clarinetist was performing so badly that one irate listener hissed, "Fool!" The conductor turned about angrily and asked, "Who called that clarinet player a fool?" The crushing answer from the front row was, "The question is not who called that clarinet player a fool, but who called that fool a clarinet player!"

An art teacher was discussing with a pupil about his work. The pupil protested, "But I am sure that

I am painting what I see." The teacher replied witheringly, "The real shock will come when you *see* what you have painted!"

The justification of practice is not in the hours expended but in the music or the picture or the manual and mental aptitude that emerges. The sole justification for discipline is in the character that results, the victory over the egocentric self, the capacity of prolonged attention to God, and the greater likeness to Christ. If these do not appear, then the disciplines have been misunderstood and misdirected.

Practice the disciplines but do not keep score. Practice and forget. Never, never compare your record with that of any other person in the world. You are not out to break any records but to break the hold things and people and the ego have upon your attention. It is not important how many times you have denied yourself but how truly you have detached yourself from yourself, and set yourself free to think of God and to love God.

Repression Vs. Discipline

These disciplines must not be confused with repression. Repression is ashamed of reality; discipline confronts reality and masters it. Repression refuses recognition to impulse and pretends that it is not there. Discipline confesses, "Yes, I want to do it, but it is not good for me or for society, therefore I will not do it."

160

Repression says of such things as anger or hate or envy, "Why, of course, I could never have any such feelings." Discipline says, "Yes, I do feel that way very strongly at times, but feelings are not going to run and ruin my life. I will control them and pray for help." Repression is ashamed of natural hungers and yearnings, and tries to thrust them out of the mind. Discipline honors the hungers and yearnings as God's gifts to our stewardship and deals with them on the conscious level.

Repression solves no problems created by impulse or emotion but only thrusts them down into the subconscious areas where they fester and fume. These conflicts become sources of anxiety, depression, and compulsions that badger the soul and destroy its peace. Discipline meets impulse and emotion with intelligence and grace and makes of them the dynamic of the good life.

The repressed person is sitting on dynamite whose impending explosion threatens his or her whole existence; the disciplined person has harnessed his or her energies to the noble deeds and redemptive service to which God calls!

The repressed person is worn out with the struggle against the impulsions and compulsions that are forever trying to get out into action. The disciplined person experiences no such weariness, for what lies below the level of awareness is not a cage of wild beasts but a corral of domesticated animals ready to help pull the load and do the work. The repressed person is a "house divided against itself"(Luke 11:17); the disciplined person is an integrated personality under the lordship of Christ.

Never having accepted self, the repressed person is always trying to hide everything that does not agree with its false ego-image, and desperately tries to remain in control. The disciplined person knows self-acceptance because of God's acceptance. The disciplined person can work together with God to change what should be changed. Repression is life-denying; discipline is life-affirming!

Bonhoeffer's Example

Certainly one of the greatest spirits of our time was Dietrich Bonhoeffer. He was brave beyond all the bravery of the battlefield as he voiced Christian convictions amid Nazi terror. Before he died a martyr at the hands of his Nazi executioner, Bonhoeffer wrote these lines, which are preserved in *The Cost of Discipleship:*

> Who am I? They often tell me
> I stepped from my cell's confinement
>   calmly, cheerfully, firmly like a
>   squire from his country house.
> Who am I? They often tell me I used to
>   speak to my warders [wardens] freely,
>   friendly, and clearly, as though it
>   were mine to command.

Who am I? They also tell me I bore the
   days of misfortune equally, smilingly,
   proudly, like one accustomed to win.
Am I then really that which other men
   tell me of?
Or am I only what I myself know of
   myself?
Restless and longing and sick, like a
   bird in a cage, struggling for breath,
   as though hands were compressing
   my throat,
      yearning for colours, for flowers, for
         the voices of birds,
      thirsting for words of kindness, for
         neighborliness,
      tossing in expectation of great events,
      powerlessly trembling for friends at
         an infinite distance,
      weary and empty at praying, at think-
         ing, at making,
      faint and ready to say farewell to all?
Who am I? This or the other?
Whom am I? They mock me, these lone-
   ly questions of mine.
Whoever I am, Thou knowest, O God,
   I am Thine.

There, in one glorious vignette, is revealed a disciplined spirit. A repressed person would have
refused to confess the yearnings, the homesick-
ness, the hungers for beauty and kindness, the

weariness at prayer, and the fainting heart that
dreaded the hangman's noose. But this honest
soul, facing to the full all within him that shrank
from martyrdom, nevertheless could walk cheerfully in prison corridors, talk freely with those
who locked him in his cell, deport himself with
smiling dignity and the grace of the crucified. That
is how true discipline works and how it manifests
itself in the life of those who know the difference
between repression and discipline.

Be Yourself

*Discipline must never be conceived as denial
or destruction of your own uniqueness.* You must
not be an imitation of Francis of Assisi, or Saint
John of The Cross, or Evelyn Underhill, or Simone
Weil, or Thomas Kelly, or Rufus Jones. God does
not want you to be like them or like anybody but
yourself. God has given you special endowments,
called you to be what nobody else has ever been
or can be, seeks from you achievements that no
one else can duplicate.

In order to reach your potential in God, there
are disciplines that your uniqueness requires for
its fulfillment. The lack of those disciplines will
impair your capacities and frustrate God's dreams
for you. The imposition of other disciplines,
which have served others well but are unsuited to
your temperament and your task, will muddle
your spirit and mar your service.

David wisely refused to wear Saul's armor. It suited neither his training nor his skill. The apostle Paul would not let his liberty be judged by another person's conscience.

Evelyn Underhill wrote to a troubled soul who was putting herself through some recommended ordeals: "Gentle aspirations! no strain and no fixed rule! Be one-tenth as kind to yourself as you were to me and you will do very nicely."

To another who felt that discipline required "a giving up," she replied: "I am not going to say you should give it up at the moment, and I could not possibly promise that doing so would bring you nearer to God. But be reasonable. Remember you hold your body and your nervous system in trust from God and must treat His property well. . . . The great task for you, as you see, is cleansing love of possessiveness, and that you are doing, and I know it is a big job which asks for real heroism."

To still another she wrote: "Don't attempt to force a complete surrender while it raises a tornado. Just acknowledge very humbly that you can not get past the tornado without His grace but that underneath it all, you do desire to give yourself, or rather to be taken from yourself into His love."

The great men and women of God, who urged discipline, nevertheless realized that the discipline must fit the person. It must not destroy but preserve individuality, not make a mimic but a master, not create a copy but an authentic character.

That does not mean the elimination of all rigor. The suiting of discipline to the individual does not imply "taking-it-easy." This is no counsel of tranquilization. Florence Allshorn wrote so pungently: "Getting rid of the self is the only means of freeing you to love . . . if we start on the way of redemption and refuse when it begins to make us suffer, whether it is our pride, or our nerves, or our comfort, we are most horribly disloyal!" We are!

Discipline—Not Bondage

What we must keep ever in mind, however, is that we are not to copy the sufferings of others, but accept the sufferings that are involved in the death of our own egocentricity. Another person's self-denial may be a picnic for us, just as surely as the other may prove to be our perdition.

The important thing in all this is to recognize that God wants each one to be an individual, an emancipated and illuminated self. Any discipline that mutilates this uniqueness is a distortion. Any practice that robs one of the capacity to be individual and free in that individuality is malpractice.

Recently I heard a courageous, adventurous, pioneering minister say to his adventuring congregation: "I want you to feel free to be yourself in Christ, to be true to your individual concept of Christ's will for you, and to feel safe among us

166

in your uniqueness!" It was a thrilling experience to hear this minister, who himself is living the disciplined life, tell his people that discipline does not mean conformity but liberty. They knew, when he said that, he was not giving them license to go their egocentric, self-willed ways but was releasing them to go Christ's way even though that way did not fit into the daring patterns of that congregation's program and life.

That is the message of this chapter. Discipline does not mean bondage but loyalty to Christ's dream for you. This book points out the lines along which many have found their deliverance. But those lines are not boundaries. They are direction signs. They have proved to be helpful to multitudes. May God bless them to your progress along the road from now to God's vast forever!

The Disciplines
Of Jesus

13
The Disciplines Of Jesus

Nothing will help us more to make of these disciplines what they should be than a continuing remembrance of Jesus Christ. Jesus was the most wisely disciplined person in history. Name the disciplines one by one, recalling His perfect illustration of their meaning and purpose:

Obedience: Jesus said, "Not my will, but thine, be done" (Luke 22:42), and, "My meat is to do the will of him that sent me, and to finish his work" (John 4:34). As Paul Tillich said, Jesus lived in unbroken unity with God and yet sought nothing for Himself by that unity.

Simplicity: Jesus lived simply. He said, "Foxes have holes, and the birds of the air have nests; but the Son of man hath not where to lay his head" (Matthew 8:20). There was no effort on His part to make an impression. He refused the spectacular and He spoke the language of the people; He gave no false impressions and kept silent when He did not know the answers: "of that day and

171

that hour knoweth no man, no, not the angels which are in heaven, neither the Son" (Mark 13:32).

Humility: Jesus said, "Why callest thou me good? There is none good but one, that is, God" (Mark 10:18). He urged others, "Take my yoke upon you, and learn of me; for I am meek and lowly in heart" (Matthew 11:29).

Frugality: Jesus knew and spoke the truth with these words: "How hard it is for those who have riches to enter the kingdom of God" (Luke 18:24 *RSV*). It is written of Jesus, "For your sakes he became poor, that ye through his poverty might be rich" (2 Corinthians 8:9). Jesus knew the secret of true wealth: "Man shall not live by bread alone, but by every word that proceedeth out of the mouth of God" ((Matthew 4:4); "They which are gorgeously apparelled, and live delicately, are in kings' courts" (Luke 7:25). Frugal in food, Jesus fasted long days in the wilderness. Frugal in sleep, He spent whole nights in prayer alone with God. Frugal in personal relationships, He loved people but could get along without them if His truth offended them. He asked His disciples, "Will ye also go away?" (John 6:67).

Generosity: Jesus gave everything to God—everything! His days and nights, His dreams and deeds, His labors and His life itself belonged to God. Jesus gave Himself wholeheartedly to people, sharing with them His truth, ministering to their souls, healing their sickness, listening to their questions. "For there were many coming and going and they had no leisure so much as to eat" (Mark 6:31); "And Jesus went about all the cities and villages, teaching in their synagogues, and preaching the gospel of the kingdom and healing every sickness. . . . But when he saw the multitudes, he was moved with compassion on them, because they fainted, and were scattered abroad, as sheep having no shepherd" (Matthew 9:35,36).

Truthfulness: Even the enemies of Christ had to say, "We know that you are true . . . you do not regard the position of men, but truly teach the way of God" (Mark 12:14 *RSV*). Deceit, evasion, double-talk, ambiguity, exaggeration, flattery, and guile never appeared in His life even when, by common strategy, they promised advantage to His selfless cause.

Purity: Only Jesus could claim not even a look in the direction of evil, no mixed motives, no service adulterated by sly, self-interest, nothing that did not fit the concept of godliness: He not only said, "Blessed are the pure in heart" (Matthew 5:8), He was that!

Charity: The apostle Paul's deathless portrayal of charity had Jesus as its model. Every quality of life that good usage calls *charity* was Christ's in abundance—gentleness, graciousness, quick forgiveness, generosity, courtesy, self-sacrifice, universality of good will, channeling God's love toward all persons—of all this Jesus was the perfect incarnation.

173

These superlative qualities of life were not all sheer native endowment. They were His because God was in Him—that is true. But God was in Him because He did what the rest of us must do—by dedication and discipline keep one's life completely open to God.

We have few records of Jesus's childhood, therefore we cannot watch His development. But we do have a significant clue. After that first thrilling visit to Jerusalem as a boy, it is said: "And he went down with them [his parents] and came to Nazareth, and was obedient to them. . . . And Jesus increased in wisdom and in stature, and in favor with God and man" (Luke 2:51,52 *RSV*).

Years later when Jesus was in the midst of His public ministry, the people who knew Him as a youth and young man were astonished. They asked each other: "Is not this the carpenter's son? Is not his mother called Mary? And his brothers James and Joseph and Simon and Judas? And are not all his sisters with us? Where then did this man get all this?" (Matthew 13:55 *RSV*).

The obvious meaning of such wonderment and question is that all the while Jesus was growing up, His growing was like that of all the other boys in the community. He had not impressed them as a little god walking the streets and visiting in their homes. First as a lad and then as a man, Jesus was going through the same disciplines and having the same battles as the rest, achieving as they achieved and experiencing the same frustrations as hindered them.

We do Jesus and ourselves a disservice if we assume that He enjoyed an inevitable inheritance or a unilateral divine endowment, involving none of the choices and training that are required by us. The captain of our salvation was made perfect through suffering—that is the New Testament analysis! (See Hebrews 2:10.) "Because he himself has suffered and been tempted, he is able to help those who are tempted" (Hebrews 2:18 *RSV*) . "In every respect [Jesus] has been tempted as we are, yet without sinning" (Hebrews 4:15 *RSV*).

If He was not tempted to drift, to self-indulgence, to egocentric aims and actions, then He has not been tempted as we are. If He has not known the rigors of discipline, of "going beyond the call of duty," of saying no day by day to what in itself is good but what stands between us and the best, then He has not suffered as we suffer.

Furthermore, Jesus insisted upon self-denial. "Whosoever will come after me, let him deny himself" (Mark 8:34)—and recognized that many will have to leave "houses or brothers or sisters or father or mother or children or lands" (Matthew 19:29 *RSV*) for His sake; His vivid analogy of cutting off the right hand or plucking out the right eye as a description of what humans must do if they are to inherit the divine (Matthew 5:29,30)— all these teachings imply that He knew by

175

personal experience the necessity and also the deep dimensions of the disciplines. No mere Lenten observance for Him! Rather a year-around detachment from all that could come between the spirit of man and the Spirit of God.

The Perfect Practice Of The Disciplines

Jesus was a disciplined soul. But see how sensible and free and discriminating and delivering was His practice of disciplines!

1. *We have warned against making discipline an end in itself. Jesus is the superb illustration of avoidance of that error.*

He fasted both from food and from companionship. Witness his forty days in the wilderness. (See Matthew 4:2.) There is no hint that He did that to break any records or to be able to boast, "I have gone off into solitude forty days at a time. I have fasted longer than any of you." He did it in order to find His Father's will for His public ministry.

Jesus did not marry. But his bachelorhood was not the result of any aversion to matrimony or any persuasion that a home could not foster holiness. And certainly it was not to impress people with his elevation above the common level! His mission required it. No person with family responsibilities could do what Jesus did.

The same thing was true of His voluntary poverty. Jesus was not proud of His lack of property. He accepted it so He might be unhampered in His concentration on discovering and proclaiming the will of God for His people.

His utter generosity was not that He might have a fanfare of trumpets sounded before Him wherever He went. But He knew only by giving Himself unreservedly to God and the people could Jesus make His life most significant for His own time and all time.

If ever disciplines were employed only as means to the noblest ends, it was in the life of Jesus of Nazareth.

2. *We have sought to distinguish between discipline and repression. How wonderfully Jesus did that!*

Jesus often had to say no to Himself and to others. But He was not ashamed to admit that He wished He might have said yes. Jesus also had to say yes to God and humankind, but He never thrust the opposing no down into His subconscious nor disowned its presence.

Jesus often went without sleep in order to be available to others and to God. But He never pretended, to Himself or to others, to be above the need of sleep. Once while His disciples were rowing against the wind on a rough sea, Jesus unashamedly and without apology laid down upon the floor of the boat and slept. Nor did He pretend that He was praying instead of sleeping!

Although wearied at times with the spiritual imperceptivity of His friends, Jesus did not pretend to relish their dullness of hearing. Jesus never acted as if further explanation of the obvious was stealing time from other people who needed Him or from other tasks that were more urgent. He fairly blurted out: "O faithless and perverse generation, how long am I to be with you? How long am I to bear with you?" (Matthew 17:17 *RSV*).

His glory was, first, that He accepted the fact of His own irritation; second, that He refused to let it determine His actions. Jesus did remain with the disciples until His mission was fulfilled, and He loved them all the more! That was discipline—facing the reality of their dullness and His emotional reaction against it, and yet nevertheless acting toward His disciples with sacrificial love.

At the end Jesus was confronted by the cross. His human nature shrank from it. Instead of repressing His reluctance, He expressed it: "Now is my soul troubled; and what shall I say? Father save me from this hour?" (John 12:27 *RSV*). Then having faced it, He also faced the summons from on high: "No, for this purpose I have come to this hour. Father, glorify thy name" (John 12:27,28 *RSV*).

The most perfectly disciplined person in history was at the same time the most free from the mischief and the miseries of repression!

3. *We have also tried to rescue discipline from the perils of patternization,* and insist that the discipline fit the person, not cramp or diminish one's

178

individuality. It should make of that person not a mimic but a master, not a copy but an authentic character. *Again, in Jesus we have the perfect example of the discipline that sets one free to be oneself as God wills.*

Jesus had great respect for Moses and the prophets. "If they hear not Moses and the prophets, neither will they be persuaded, though one rose from the dead"(Luke 16:31). But He did not hesitate to differ from these revered heroes of Israel's past. Jesus often cited to His hearers their own great traditions of ethics and religion: "Think not that I have come to abolish the law and the prophets . . . but to fulfill them" (Matthew 5:17 *RSV*).

Christ's creative interpretation so angered the authorities that they plotted to abolish Him! His disciplines did not make Him an imitator but a liberator: "Ye have heard that it was said by them of old . . . but I say unto you" (Matthew 5:21-22). How much we are indebted to Him for His freedom thus to think and to speak. The most disciplined man of His generation was also the most unique and the most daring.

Nor did His disciplines issue in rigidity and monotony. Jesus could and did fast, but He also could and did feast. Critics strongly objected, and Jesus was aware of their objection: "John came neither eating nor drinking, and they say, 'He has a demon'; the Son of man came eating and drinking, and they say, 'Behold, a glutton and a drunkard, a friend of tax collectors and sinners!' ''(Matthew 11:18,19 *RSV*). There was no real contradiction at this point except in the eyes of the conformists.

Jesus fasted for the glory of God and for His service to people. He dined also for the glory of God and the service of people. Jesus could go off into the wilderness alone when that was necessary for the realization of the nature of His mission; He could sit down with publicans and sinners when that was necessary for the fulfillment of His mission.

Jesus, happily for us and for His mission, did not conceive of discipline as a straitjacket. He made of it an athlete's training for the wise and effective diversification of choice and behavior.

At Any Cost

One of the sad misinterpretations of discipline has been that it is an unhealthy exaltation, almost an idolization of suffering. Bernard Shaw's biting comment aptly described that attitude and the practice of some very earnest people: "Many assumed that they were the most religious when they were the most uncomfortable."

Browning's Caliban felt that his God was likely to be very displeased with any happiness among earth's creatures. So he did his dancing in the dark where he would not be seen. When the sun came up he pretended to be most miserable: "The best way to escape his ire is not to seem happy."

The history of mysticism is replete with the stories of sincere God-seekers, who, not content with the sufferings life normally brings, invented means of self-torture, hair shirts, girdles of iron, stones in their shoes, flagellations so severe that their blood ran, fasting to the point of emaciation!

There was none of that in Jesus, nor is there any in this book. The disciplines recommended here lie in the practice of virtue—obedience, simplicity, humility, frugality, generosity, truthfulness, purity, and charity. That is the search, not for suffering but for the Kingdom of God. The Kingdom of God is these and other virtues. "The kingdom of God is not meat and drink; but righteousness" (Romans 14:17).

Most serious people recognize that. Many earnestly seek it. Their failure is in not seeking *at any cost*. It is when it begins to *cost* that the real discipline begins. That is the discipline herein portrayed and commended.

> For all through life I see a cross
> Where sons of God yield up their
> breath;
> There is no gain except by loss,
> There is no life except through death!

Appendix

The Disciplined Order of Christ

Under the leadership of Dr. Albert E. Day in the summer of 1945, one hundred and twenty clergy and laypersons met at Albion College in Michigan to seek God's guidance at the close of World War II. Together they caught a vision of what life can be under Christ—a life of ethical sensitivity, spiritual insight, social concern, and heroic devotion to the Kingdom of God. To those gathered at Albion, it seemed that nothing less than such a life revealed through Jesus Christ would be adequate for the moral confusion, personal dilemmas, and social crises of the modern world. To foster such a life, the Disciplined Order of Christ was founded.

A unique feature of the D.O.C. is the practice of these seven spiritual disciplines with an annual renewal and accountability:

1. Setting aside a daily time for private prayer, meditation, serious study of the Bible and other great religious literature.

2. Personal commitment to a lifestyle which emphasizes obedience, simplicity, humility, frugality, generosity, truthfulness, purity, and charity.

3. Participation in a small group fellowship for the sharing of insights, problems, joys, and for prayer and social action.

4. Active involvement in the ministry of an organized church.

5. Witnessing their faith to others and sharing the good news of the Kingdom of God.

6. Recognition of God's gracious gifts of body, mind, spirit, and all material things, and of their obligation to use these gifts in service to others.

7. The discipline of ecumenical fellowship recognizing that all persons are worthy of Christian love.

The Disciplined Order of Christ is a spiritual movement of persons who are seriously committed to disciplines and practices required for growing in the mind and spirit of Christ.

For further information contact:

DISCIPLINED ORDER OF CHRIST
PO BOX 3681
FLORENCE SC 29502